CREDIT SCORE
POWER

A VIEW INTO
THE MISUNDERSTOOD RULES OF CREDIT
AND WHAT MAKES FOR
THE BEST SCORES

TRACY BECKER

iUniverse, Inc.
Bloomington

Copyright © 2011 by Tracy Becker

All rights reserved. No part of this book may be used or reproduced by any means, graphic, electronic, or mechanical, including photocopying, recording, taping or by any information storage retrieval system without the written permission of the publisher except in the case of brief quotations embodied in critical articles and reviews.

iUniverse books may be ordered through booksellers or by contacting:

iUniverse
1663 Liberty Drive
Bloomington, IN 47403
www.iuniverse.com
1-800-Authors (1-800-288-4677)

Because of the dynamic nature of the Internet, any web addresses or links contained in this book may have changed since publication and may no longer be valid. The views expressed in this work are solely those of the author and do not necessarily reflect the views of the publisher, and the publisher hereby disclaims any responsibility for them.

Any people depicted in stock imagery provided by Thinkstock are models, and such images are being used for illustrative purposes only.

Certain stock imagery © Thinkstock.

ISBN: 978-1-4620-0717-2 (sc)
ISBN: 978-1-4620-0718-9 (ebook)

Library of Congress Control Number: 2011904556

Printed in the United States of America

iUniverse rev. date: 06/17/2011

Contents

CHAPTER ONE
Who Are the Credit Bureaus, and What Do They Do?   1

CHAPTER TWO
Credit Scores and the Credit-Scoring Systems   15

CHAPTER THREE
Shopping for a Mortgage or Loan   37

CHAPTER FOUR
Having the Best Credit   56

CHAPTER FIVE
Negative Information   71

CHAPTER SIX
Examples of Financial Stress   101

CHAPTER SEVEN
Credit Monitoring and Identity Protection   111

Chapter One

Who Are the Credit Bureaus, and What Do They Do?

Credit-reporting agencies were created in the 1900s, when people started moving across the country. At this time, it was difficult to track consumer credit histories, since they could default on loans, move easily from place to place, and just begin again in a new area. Within the United States, there began to be many more banks and lenders, so payment histories were harder to track for each individual. In the past, there would be a local lender who could see each individual's full credit history, since they had control of all the lending. That lender being the only available choice for borrowing money made it easy to regulate payment patterns. Because of these growth changes, the need for an entity that could provide all of an individual's or business' credit history, no matter where they were located at any given time, was paramount.

Credit bureaus, also known as credit-reporting agencies (CRAs), are nongovernmental agencies that collect and sell information. There is more than one agency because, like most businesses, they compete for profits. Two of them are public, and one is a private company. For the most part, the information they provide includes histories of creditworthiness, showing how business and consumers rate in terms of their ability to meet debt obligations. The CRAs provide many other services related to gathering information, statistics, and selling information to companies for marketing purposes.

Personal credit profiles provide creditors, collectors, and solicitors with a view of a consumer's history for a period of seven to twenty years. Generally, positive information can remain for the period it is open and active and can be removed after two years of inactivity (closing of account). Although information does not have to be reported for longer than this period, many creditors will leave it on the report indefinitely. Negative information generally remains for seven to ten years, depending on what it is. I speak more about this and the exceptions in later chapters. The three major consumer credit bureaus that supply the majority of consumer credit are TransUnion, Equifax, and Experian.

TransUnion
TransUnion has been in business since 1968, with headquarters in Chicago. It is a private company that recently sold more than half of its shares.[1] The Pritzker family, who owns Trans Union and much more, reported that they sold 51 percent of their stake to a private equity firm, Madison Dearborn,

> Personal credit profiles provide creditors, collectors, and solicitors with a view of a consumer's history for a period of more than seven years.

in 2010. This sale was the result of many disputes within the family, after which they agreed their $15 billion empire, which included TransUnion, would be divided by 2011. TransUnion is the smallest of the three reporting bureaus, supporting more than fifty thousand customers on five continents and more than five hundred million consumers across the globe.[1]

Equifax

Equifax was founded in 1898 by two brothers—Cator and Guy Woolford, a bank employee and an attorney, respectively—who started compiling information reported by creditors on the history of payment patterns of their shoppers. They published their findings in the form of a guide, which they sold to merchants for twenty-five dollars. They also sold credit reports on individual consumers. It was such a success that it has grown to be the business it is today.

Equifax is a public company that has been gathering information for consumers and businesses for over one hundred years. It employs over seven thousand people in fifteen countries. Equifax focuses on solutions for business and provides consumers with credit reports as well. The business solutions Equifax provides include information and lists to help a business market to the right consumer. Since information is power, the recording of individuals' credit histories and personal information makes the bureau a valuable resource for business.

---

1 Yerak, Becky, and Wernau, Julie, April 29, 2010, *Chicago Tribune*, http://articles.chicagotribune.com.

Experian

In 1996, the old Experian (which was called TRW) was combined with the CCN Group by GUS plc, the British conglomerate. The CCN Group was Europe's largest information bureau. Everyone recognizes the name TRW, and some consumers still use the name, not realizing the company is no longer TRW but Experian. Over the ten-year period after the two companies merged, GUS developed and strengthened Experian. Then, in 2006, GUS demerged the two, and Experian became an independent company. Experian is a public company that employs about fifteen thousand people and provides data and services to clients in more than sixty-five countries.

On a consumer level, the three CRAs serve as a library of information about how patterns of payments reflect individual credit histories. Creditors constantly provide updated and new information changes in credit history, whether positive, negative, accurate, or in many cases, inaccurate. This information is compiled and resold to members who make decisions about approving credit applications. There are hundreds if not thousands of regional bureaus across the United States under contract or owned by one of the three bureaus mentioned.

Credit Information Uses

Credit bureaus also offer services to businesses, helping companies across the globe manage risks and rewards related to lending to consumers and other businesses. These services include:

- Credit Services: They maintain databases that hold information about all consumers on a national, and in many cases, global level.

- Decision Analytics: They offer analytical tools and skills that help give organizations support to make better decisions.

- Marketing Services: Through their marketing services, they help clients find and keep customers.

- Interactive: They open communications between consumers and businesses by providing many services, including e-mail, telephone, direct-response mail, and text. This enables businesses to develop a larger client base.

- Protection Products: The bureaus also sell products that allow consumers to manage and protect their personal credit profiles and to view a variety of credit score models.

Many businesses use lists of specific types of consumers who fit into their desired category of clients. For example, Capital One offers a 0 percent interest rate credit card to a consumer who lives in an area where the average income is over $90,000. They are looking for a consumer with five other lines of credit with at least 40 percent of balance to limit ratio on credit card debt, a mortgage, a student loan, and an automobile loan or lease. This type of consumer may be the best choice for the creditor issuing this card, since this consumer is more likely to transfer high balances over to this card. Capital One can go to the CRAs and request a consumer list based on these specifications.

Use of qualification-specific lists could also work for a company that is negotiating tax debt or looking for potential foreclosure candidates. CRAs can supply a list of all consumers with unpaid tax liens or borrowers who have four to six consecutive late payments on their current mortgage. A creditor might be looking to market to students looking for used textbooks. In this case, a list might be requested of consumers in a certain age range with open student loans. They might look for a lower-income address as well. These are just a few examples of some of the ways these lists might work.

After speaking with thousands of bankers and consumers, one question that often comes up is about being solicited by various companies. These companies, such as debt settlement, credit card, mortgage, loan modification, and even credit restoration firms, buy lists of specific categories of consumers from CRAs. This is a huge source of revenue for credit bureaus (Experian, TransUnion, and Equifax). Since their business is gathering detailed information about all consumers—including their spending habits, debt accumulation, home ownership status, and much more—it makes perfect sense they would use this information to make more profits. These lists are available to any business for the right price.

How often have we been interrupted by a phone call, at the worst possible moment, to find out we are approved for the "opportunity" to have our debt settled for a fraction of the price, refinance our mortgage, restore our credit, buy life or car insurance at better prices, and much more? I have heard of businesses getting these solicitations as well. They come in many forms, such as regular mail, e-mail, and, of course, those phone calls. These days, many people keep a shredder near the desk where they read mail, so they can securely dispose of all the credit card offers (and more).

So, now you know how that telemarketer who called you last week might have gotten your information. How the insurance company that sent you a promotional letter knew you just bought a new home or car or even had a car accident. You can imagine the power and money these lists could provide to any business.

After giving you a picture of the negatives associated with these solicitations, it is important to understand the positives, too. Many times we learn more about what is available, scam or valid, and are given new ideas about our choices when we engage these solicitors. I personally learn about many scams by listening and evaluating what I hear and read from this information. Of course, that includes the radio advertisements, but the difference is we have more control over the radio ads, and the information is presented to us by turning on the radio as opposed to getting literature or phone calls directed at us specifically as individuals.

A variety of consumers call us to ask questions about their choices after speaking with companies that have contacted them through these lists. Consistently, they are asking for recommendations from their CPAs, financial planners, mortgage experts, or trusted friends who refer them to us for advice. When interviewing these consumers, we uncover the fact that the information they are given by the sales representative is usually only a portion of the truth. Many consequential factors are withheld, such as the tax ramification of settling debt, ratios of savings, decrease in their credit score, time it takes for their credit to recover, and so on. It is helpful to remember that in most cases these calls have motivated consumers to pursue more information about the choice they have been offered and often lead them to a better solution for their situation if they do their homework.

Opting Out
If you would still like to opt out of being solicited via CRAs, I am providing information taken directly from the Federal Trade Commission's site, www.ftc.gov/bcp/edu/pubs/consumer/alerts/alt063.shtm:

"The credit bureaus offer a toll-free number that enables you to 'opt-out' of having pre-approved credit offers sent to you for five years. Call 1-888-5-OPTOUT (567-8688) or visit www.optoutprescreen.com for more information. When you call, you'll be asked for personal information, including your home telephone number, your name, and your Social Security number. The information you provide is confidential and will be used only to process your request to opt out of receiving pre-screened offers of credit. In addition, you can notify the three major credit bureaus that you do not want personal information about you shared for promotional purposes—an important step toward eliminating unsolicited mail. Write your own letter or use the information (SEE BELOW) to limit the amount of information the credit bureaus will share about you. Send your letter to each of the three major credit bureaus:

Experian
901 West Bond
Lincoln, NE 68521
Attn: Consumer Services Department

TransUnion
Name Removal Option
P.O. Box 505
Woodlyn, PA 19094

Equifax, Inc.
Options
P.O. Box 740123
Atlanta, GA 30374-0123

"(Please reconfirm these addresses if you are using this info after 2011.)

"The letter should have the date, your full name, Social Security number, date of birth, address and previous address (if you have moved within the last two years). It should state: I request to have my name removed from your marketing list.

Attaching proof of address and your Social Security number is a good idea as well.

"Do Not Call
"The federal government has created the National Do Not Call Registry—a free, easy way to reduce the telemarketing calls you get at home. To register your phone number or to get information about the registry, visit www.donotcall.gov, or call 1-888-382-1222 from the phone number you want to register. You will get fewer telemarketing calls within 31 days of registering your number. Telephone numbers on the registry will only be removed when they are disconnected and reassigned, or when you choose to remove a number from the registry.

"The Direct Marketing Association's (DMA) Mail Preference Service lets you opt out of receiving unsolicited commercial mail from many national companies for five years. When you register with this service (for a $1.00 fee), your name will be put on a 'delete' file and made available to direct-mail marketers. However, your registration will not stop mailings from organizations that do not use the DMA's Mail Preference Service. To register with DMA's Mail Preference Service, go to www.dmachoice.org.

"E-mail

"The DMA also has an E-mail Preference Service to help you reduce unsolicited commercial e-mails. To opt out of receiving unsolicited commercial e-mail from DMA members, visit www.dmachoice.org/EMPS. Your online request will be effective for five years."

Business Credit

Business credit is based on a company's employer identification number (EIN), its payment history, and financial reports. One of the biggest differences between business and consumer credit is that the late payments can affect business credit more, depending on how high the debt is in comparison with other open accounts. If late payments are made to a vendor owed $20,000 in debt and there are other vendors with higher debt owed, the score will be affected less. If a business is late paying a vendor with the highest debt on the business's credit report, the scores plummet. Payment history is dependent on dollar value of the debt for each vendor. The higher the debt owed to the vendor, the heavier the dip in score if a late payment occurs.

Business Scores

We will discuss personal scores, such as FICO, in the next chapter, but credit bureaus also create scores for businesses. There are four main scores discussed in this section that are related to Dun & Bradstreet Credit: paydex, financial stress, commercial credit, and Dun & Bradstreet (D&B) rating. Dun & Bradstreet was one of the first companies created to provide information for business-to-business decision making. As lenders needed risk data when underwriting loans and credit extensions for consumers, it makes perfect sense there would also be a need for the same type of information when deciding to lend money or give credit extensions to businesses. In 1841, the first CRA was created with business credit histories as the focus. It was a businessman named Lewis Tappan who set up shop in New York. Eight years later, he turned over his business to Benjamin Douglass, who continued to build the company's reputation. In 1859, Douglass turned the company over to Robert Graham Dun. In 1849, John M. Bradstreet opened a competing company in Ohio. The companies were fierce competitors until they merged in 1933 to become Dun & Bradstreet, known today as the oldest and most popular source of business credit reporting.[2] Dun & Bradstreet merged with TransUnion in 2010 and has been using the vast consumer credit bureau's information to build upon its already sophisticated programs and products. It has fine-tuned many of its scores and indexes.

Paydex

For a business, one of the most important scores is its D&B Paydex score. Knowing what this number is and having the ability to increase it can mean acquiring financing needed to start or grow your business. These abilities can make the difference in achieving your business goals or losing your business. Dun & Bradstreet's definition of the Paydex score is: "The D&B Paydex score is its unique, dollar-weighted numerical indicator of how a firm paid its bills over the past year, based on trade experiences reported to D&B by various vendors. The D&B Paydex score ranges from one to one hundred, with higher scores indicating better payment performance."[3]

---

[2] Dun & Bradstreet website, January 2011, http://www.dnb.com/about-dnb/history/14909191-1.html.

[3] Dun & Bradstreet website, January 2011, https://www.dnb.com/product/birgloss.htm.

A strong Paydex score can help give a business access to credit lines for marketing efforts, buying or leasing needed equipment, and getting the supplies required to land bigger clients and higher revenues. Obviously, if the score is low, the opposite will occur.

The Paydex score reflects a company's history of payments to creditors or vendors. It is rare to see a score as high as one hundred. An excellent score would be an eighty. An eighty indicates all bills are being paid promptly. On the other end of the spectrum, a score of sixty is considered low and represents late payments. Below a sixty could mean many defaults or very little credit history.

Paying your vendors on time will not give you as high a score as paying vendors early. If you pay immediately and don't have open judgments or collections, your Paydex score may be closer to the top. This also depends on how many vendors you have.

Financial Stress Score
D&B's financial stress score was designed to help predict a business's potential for failure. It is designed to predict the likelihood that a company will, over the next twelve months, obtain legal relief from creditors or cease operations without paying all creditors in full. The score uses the full range of D&B information, including financials, comparative financial ratios, payment trends, public filings, and demographic data.[4]

4   Dun & Bradstreet website, January 2011, http://smallbusiness.dnb.com/glossaries/financial-stress-score.

Commercial Credit–Scoring System

The commercial credit–scoring model is based on the observed characteristics of hundreds of thousands of businesses in D&B's database. D&B's commercial credit score is designed to predict the likelihood that a company will pay its bills in a severely delinquent manner (ninety days or more past terms), obtain legal relief from creditors, or cease operations without paying all creditors in full over the next twelve months.

D&B Rating

The D&B rating can help you quickly assess a firm's size and composite credit appraisal based on information in a company's interim or fiscal balance sheet and an overall evaluation of the firm's creditworthiness.[5]

Many of these scores and ratings seem somewhat redundant. We also know that when one score increases most of the rest improve as well. They are all affected similarly by both good and bad updates on the credit profile.

---

5   Dun & Bradstreet website, January 2011, http://www.dnb.com/report/dnb-rating/15058845-1.html.

Chapter Two

Credit Scores and the Credit-Scoring Systems

The Effects of Business Credit Scores and Indexes

As the economy changed in 2008, banks and vendors became more rigid in extending financing and credit. Since so many businesses failed during that period, more vendors and potential customers began to look for more transparency before signing on the dotted line. Small businesses saw the need to be proactive in protecting their very important credit asset. To be safe, companies need to keep scores and indexes at their best in all environments, since they can make the difference between a company's ability to fail or succeed and to grow and prosper.

One of our clients, a fast-growing provider of network and IT solutions, was caught in a frustrating negative cycle. Since existing clients delayed making payments on open invoices due to the economy, it caused a domino effect of slow payments to vendors for our client. With the increasing popularity of potential clients evaluating their business credit to make decisions for future contracts, plus the fluctuations in their credit scores, the IT company was concerned it was losing future income sources. It was agreed they needed the service of daily credit monitoring and improvement to offset the dilemma of the current credit problem. Now, with credit monitoring, as soon as an issue arises, it is addressed and scores are maintained if not increased.

Another concern for local and national businesses is the risk of losing current or future positions as supplier to major companies. Some larger corporations, like Wal-Mart, have restrictive score requirements for suppliers. In 2010, Wal-Mart wouldn't even look twice at potential suppliers with a risk rating of above a 6 on their Dun & Bradstreet credit profiles. Once scores fail to meet necessary requirements, current suppliers can find their orders cancelled and products pulled off the racks. Many business owners are in a panic after learning they have been rejected from their existing position. The causes vary from cases as minor as bookkeeper errors in making timely payments to situations as major as receivables that are uncollectable and bills that cannot be paid on time. Once the damage is done, it is an uphill battle with the full realization of the consequence a great burden at best. Many businesses lose potential clients and others could wind up losing credit lines that are essential to keep the business alive. Another credit challenge we have seen affecting small businesses is when credit scores are in current excellent standing but have shown negative fluctuations over the past 12-24 months. When companies apply for financing on many leases, various types of software, machinery, and equipment some creditors will reject applicants due to varied and dramatic score movement over a period of time. The history of the score movement paints a picture of a volatile paying experience which in many cases reflects a potential for higher risk of default.

A local doctor in private practice for three years was rejected for new equipment due to poor score history. Since he had left a larger practice to go into private practice, he was focused on building his new business and had paid no attention to his credit. He needed some expensive equipment and decided to check his credit profile, expecting it to be fine. To his surprise and disappointment, there was a collection showing over a seven-month period. Besides the collection, he only had one other vendor listed on the report. Although the collection was an error and Dun & Bradstreet agreed to remove it from his profile, the history of the collection was still visible. His Paydex Score improved to an 80, which is considered excellent. But, when the financing company reviewed the pattern of payment history, they found a 45 Paydex Score over the seven-month period the collection was visible. With his poor score history, even though his current score was great, he could not get the financing he needed under his business name. The doctor had to sign personally for the equipment. Luckily for him, his personal credit scores were excellent and he was approved.

Being proactive and making sure business credit is managed by a professional or someone within the company who can efficiently and responsibly handle this task can save enormous financial cost and stress. It is essential for small business owners to stay abreast of current score requirements. In most economies, sources providing cutting-edge information can make a world of difference.

Personal credit scores are very confusing to the majority of consumers. They don't realize how many variations of credit scores there are. Not only is the average consumer perplexed, many professionals who deal with credit and finance have trouble sorting through the massive amount of information and constant changes. To understand the many types of scores, we must remember facts. Scoring is a profit-generating business; there are many kinds of lenders out there and many reasons credit scores are used to evaluate a consumer.

Credit scores are important for a variety of reasons. Since a credit score is a reflection of a consumer's worth as a credit risk, it can sway a decision by a lender as to what interest rate will be paid on all kinds of financing. These include mortgages, credit cards, lines of credit, overdraft on a checking account (since these accounts are treated the same as credit cards and are charged interest when used), business loans, personal loans, home-equity loans, and some forms of student loans. With a high credit score, you may pay 4 percent interest on a credit card as opposed to 24 percent. It could be the difference between 4.25 percent and 8 percent interest on a $500,000 mortgage. That difference correlates into hundreds and thousands of dollars of savings or costs over the life of that loan. You can imagine how many millions can be saved over fifteen to thirty years, depending on the size of the loan.

Besides saving money on a loan or credit card, a score could be so low that it causes the lender to decline a consumer for a credit card or mortgage. This rejection could be the difference between a college education, a successful business, or a lovely home in a great area and school district. You can see how the right score can change lives dramatically. Credit scores are a powerful vehicle and tool to enhance your personal life and business.

> A credit score is a number that reflects the credit risk of a consumer or business.

A credit score is a numerical representation of information on an individual's credit reports. It reflects the credit risk, or worthiness, of a consumer or business based on a statistical analysis of the credit profile of that individual or entity.

There are many credit scores. When it comes to personal credit reports, each CRA, no matter what score is used, will have its own numerical score that represents the information found on the individual report. Each bureau can have varied information on the same consumer's credit history. When a creditor reports information to a bureau, the creditor is charged a fee for updating the report. Many smaller creditors, looking to cut costs, will choose to report only to one or two of the three bureaus. Besides the inconsistency of the information creditors report to the CRAs, there is also the problem of balance updates being recorded at different times by the bureaus. When a creditor reports balance updates, it does not mean the bureaus update that information at exactly the same time.

For example:

Equifax updates a balance change on day 1.
Experian doesn't update until day 5.
TransUnion updates on day 7.

If the bank from which the consumer is applying for a mortgage pulls the credit profiles on day 3, the reports will reflect different scores from each bureau. This can be very confusing and show an inaccurate picture of a consumer's score.

This kind of inconsistent score representation may make you wonder why scores were created in the first place. Back in the 1960s, Americans had become more mobile; consumers were traveling more and more from state to state. Lenders had to rely heavily on information they received from the credit bureaus, since interviewing applicants in person was not always possible. The credit bureaus would collect data secretly, and some of the data collected on individuals was often based on hearsay and misinformation. For example, they would ask a representative from the Welcome Wagon to report back with details on the clothing, furnishings, and quality of an individual's character and personality. Since the bureaus were reporting enormous amounts of misinformation, bad decisions were being made. To make things worse, the credit bureaus were also under no legal obligation to allow consumers to see their credit records.

As time went on and more consumers borrowed money to buy homes, the government started to investigate racial discrimination cases regarding home loans. Data collection practices were analyzed and laws enacted to protect consumers and allow them to see and correct errors in their credit histories. The Fair Credit Reporting Act (FCRA) forced the CRAs to clean up inaccuracies. Once the CRAs started gathering more reliable information, lenders began to depend more on their data and less on the gut feelings of local underwriters. Since Congress was pressuring lenders about discrimination practices, the banking industry required a fair and objective measurement of credit worthiness that would protect them from being sued. Fair, Isaac and Company (FICO) took advantage of this need for a tool that could quantify a consumer's risk level by developing a numerical score based solely on the information gathered by the CRAs. This is how FICO scores came about in the 1980s.[6]

FICO Score

FICO provides a risk score tabulated by using the information on your Equifax, TransUnion, and Experian credit reports. This score is used by banks, insurance companies (car, homeowner, life, and more), real estate agencies, collection agencies, mortgage brokers, car lenders, boat lenders, employers, landlords, credit card companies—and the list goes on. FICO also offers its score to the general public for a fee as well. The score ranges from a 300 to 850; the higher the score, the lower the risk for a lender to approve funding.

---

6 Fico Forum, March 2007, http//ficoforums.myfico.com.

Factors that are taken into account in determining FICO and all other scores that relate to personal credit are:

- Payment history: have there been late payments, do you pay immediately, or do you pay on time?

- How much credit is available?

- What are the ratios of revolving credit balance to limits?

- How long have you had your credit?

- How recently have you opened a credit account?

- Last date of activity on your accounts.[7]

We will get more in depth on these topics in chapter 4.

Within the FICO scores sold to lenders are different names that represent each bureau's FICO score for the information collected on the consumer. For the most part, Experian calls it Fair Isaac or FICO, TransUnion calls it Empirica, and Equifax calls it Beacon, but sometimes you see FICO on two of the three reports. The reporting agencies rebranded the names of the FICO score when it relates to the different agencies. There are also variations to the FICO score as well:

- FICO Classic 04

---

[7] FICO website, October 2010, http://www.myfico.com/Credit-Education.

- FICO 08
- FICO Classic

Other scores sold by FICO for various purposes include FICO Credit Capacity and FICO Expansion Score.

Within each variation, there are different models that are chosen by each lender through a smaller CRA. Bankers call these smaller CRAs "pulling services." They specifically sell the score to the lender. The pulling service is a third party that gets the info from the three reporting agencies: Experian, TransUnion, and Equifax. They process this information through the FICO scoring formula and model and deliver the score to the institution paying them a fee for the data. Just like any business, if you limit yourself to one product, it can inhibit your profits. When FICO offers many variations, with different reasoning behind the choices, it gives FICO more opportunities to sell and make profits, while giving their clients more specifically tailored products that can help decipher risk.

CRAs also offer their own scores to the general public for educational purposes. They are PLUS scores, the National Score Index, and Vantage scores; Equifax, in 2010, created the Equifax score.

PLUS Scores
Plus scores are only offered to the general public for educational reasons and, of course, for credit bureaus to make profits.

Lenders do not use these scores at all. This means that if you order a PLUS score, it will have no value as an indicator of your mortgage score. These scores may be based on the same indicators as FICO, but each indicator may have a different weight that affects the score. Here are the PLUS score indicators: [8]

- Your history of late payments
- Non-payments
- Current level of debt
- Types of credit accounts
- Length of credit history
- Number of credit inquiries
- History of applying for credit

All scores are affected by payment patterns, age of credit, new credit, balances, and amount of credit, but FICO may be affected more by high balances than are PLUS scores. PLUS scores range from 330 to 830 and can be twenty to forty points higher than FICO scores.

National Score Index

The National Score Index, also called the National Risk Score (NRS), measures your risk level compared with all consumers

---

8 http://www.nationalscoreindex.com/CreditTools_CreditScores_01.aspx.

across the country. Some real estate agents use this score when evaluating potential tenants on behalf of landlords.

Experian claims its NRS is easy to understand, since its range is from 0 to 1,000. The lower the score, the lower the risk. This is the reverse of the scores most of us work with today. Right now, if you have an 800 FICO score, you are in the top tier and deserve the lowest risk rates and most favorable view from any landlord or lender. If you had an 800 score with the NRS, you would have an 80 percent chance of default in the next twenty-four months! This is very high and would, therefore, make you a terrible credit risk. Most likely, you would be turned down for any financing or approval on a lease. It would be like having a 459 FICO score.

To come up with the most accurate "predictive characteristics," Experian evaluated hundreds and thousands of credit profiles over a two-year period. Some of the score's features are predicting the probability of derogatory credit patterns, including charge-offs, repossessions, foreclosures, collections, and bankruptcies. It uses eight scorecards based on an individual's past credit profiles that include amount of credit history, length of credit history, and past payment performance. An individual's score is based on a twenty-four-month performance period and ranges from 0 to 1,000 (there is an option to have the score formulated to be compatible with current scores and put into a 360 to 840 score range).[9]

---

9 National Risk Score website, October 2010, http://www.nationalscoreindex.com/AboutScoreIndex.aspx.

The NRS not only gives a score but also flags high-risk accounts so that landlords and lenders can look more deeply into the consumer's history. The score is also geared toward companies that are combing through consumers to find prospects. Experian claims, "Using multiple scorecard technology further enhance[s] the model's predictive power. This state-of-the-art technology segments prospects into groups having similar credit histories. Scores are calculated from scorecards developed specifically for each group. This allows detailed analysis of the predictive variables that vary among subpopulations and enables more accurate credit evaluation."[10] The score groups consumers with similar credit histories and then calculates how they compare from "scorecards" developed specifically for each group. This scorecard aspect seems to be used primarily for organizations that are looking for specific prospects. From what I read, the score is popular for marketing, as well.

Experian's main pitch for the NRS score is decision making and discrimination. Experian says, "With the National Risk Model, you can consistently make objective credit decisions. Because the model was empirically and statistically derived from a random sample of credit histories, your chance of making discriminatory decisions is reduced."[11] This makes sense for landlords in deciding on a potential tenant application. The laws are clear that discrimination could cost a landlord dearly, so the choice to use a score like this has its merits.

---

10   Experian Information Systems, 2001, http://www.kewaneecreditbureau.com/National.Risk.Model.pdf.
11   Experian Information Systems, 2001, http://www.kewaneecreditbureau.com/National.Risk.Model.pdf.

Vantage Score

Vantage score is a joint venture backed by the three CRAs. The score was created in 2006 by a third-party group that was organized by the CRA's. Even though the group is supposed to be separate from the CRAs, it is funded by them.[12] If this score becomes popular, it may make you wonder if it is going to give the CRAs too much power.

The Vantage score was created to educate the general public and to compete directly with FICO by selling to lenders as well. After watching FICO make a fortune selling scores, Experian decided to ask for a piece of the profits, since FICO was using its information in tabulating the scores for sale to the general public. After Experian requested a percentage of FICO profits, a negotiation between the two companies took place, and FICO said no! In February 2009, Experian declared it would no longer allow FICO the use of its information to sell Experian FICO scores to the consumer. If you went to myfico.com to order your FICO scores, you would no longer be able to buy your Experian FICO score. Although the Vantage score was created in 2006, it was in 2009 that the Vantage score was heavily marketed and really began to compete with the FICO score.

The Vantage score is a bit more complex than the FICO scores and uses current economic trends to evaluate the scores as well. It breaks down and catego-

> The Vantage score uses current economic trends to evaluate the scores as well. It breaks down and categorizes different types of revolving credit.

---

12 Vantage Score website, 2010, http://www.vantagescore.com.

rizes different types of revolving credit. For example, instead of having overdraft on a checking account, home-equity loans, and credit cards lumped into the same group (revolving credit), each is viewed separately. This, they claim, will help define the algorithms of the score in a more accurate light.[13] If you are looking at a FICO score, to date, each of these categories is considered revolving credit. Revolving credit weights more heavily on the scores, since it is the only credit you can charge the maximum and pay the minimum. It affects the score more since it is the credit we, as consumers, manage the most. It gives the score a more detailed view of our ability to control and use our credit.

Vantage views each type of revolving credit separately. For example, if you have high home equity balances but your credit card debt is low, the score would reflect the difference. In contrast, the FICO score would drop if any or all of your revolving credit balances with limits were high. This is one of the differences in the score. Some other distinctions of difference are authorized credit card holders. If you are not the primary on a credit card, it will not be considered in the tabulation of your Vantage score. This could be a good and bad thing. If you have very little credit and need your score to increase, being put on a relative or close friend's credit card as an authorized user could dramatically increase or decrease your FICO score.

The length of this credit and past paying patterns will define the affect on the score. For example, if I had one car lease, two

---

13 Vantage Score website, 2010, http://www.vantagescore.com/faqs/2010.

credit cards opened in the past year, and one student loan with a late payment from two years ago, my score might be around a 602. If I was added to my husband's ten-year-old American Express account (with great paying patterns and low balance), my score could increase sixty points or more. If the same thing happened on the Vantage score, it would not make a difference; the score would view the authorized account as invisible.

To give you some insight into the numerical difference of these scores, if all things were equal, a FICO score of 750 could translate into a Vantage score of 850 to 901, with a letter grade. It is hard to compare the two, since Vantage has different categories of consumers, and in each category, there are different risk levels. Vantage believes its scores are a clearer view of a consumer's risk level and less biased. The CRA's are still trying to get the Vantage score accepted and used by the mortgage banking industry, but to date, FICO continues to be the leader. You can still get all three FICO scores (including Experian FICO) but only through a third party. A third party would be considered a mortgage banker or a real estate broker.

The Vantage score also claims to be able to have less disparity among the three CRAs but does not explain clearly how that is possible. It seems there are some really good ideas and valuable attributes to this scoring system, but it will only be clear when it starts to be used by banks more consistently. The score runs between 501 and 990 and has a letter grade rating from A to F. An A grade and a 990 score would be the best and lowest-risk consumers.

Consumer Score Ranges

Now that we know more about many scores and how they are weighted, we need to understand the numerical values. What is considered a great score in one scoring system may be a terrible score in another.

FICO Scores: 300–850

- A great score for a consumer in 2010 would be anything above a 740, and if you are over an 800, you have amazing credit.

- A 720 is good but not great.

- Below a 680, you can still get some types of financing, like FHA mortgages.

- Anything under a 620 is poor credit.

> If you would like to review your credit profiles, you can get them all free once each year.

PLUS Scores: 330–830

- Scores can be forty points higher than FICO scores.

- Taking this into account, a 740 PLUS could put you in a different category than a 740 FICO score. The 740 PLUS score would be considered average at best for your FICO score. This would cost more money in interest for a mortgage loan. The difference in score could equal a cost of $100,000 or more, depending on the size of the loan, over the life of a loan!

Vantage Scores: 501–990

- Besides a numerical score, it has a letter grade rating from A to F.
- An A grade and a 990 score would be the best and lowest-risk consumers.

This score could be as much as one hundred to one hundred fifty points higher than the FICO score.

National Risk Scores: 0–1,000

- This score is the only one in which the lower score is better.
- This is usually used by landlords.

There are new credit scores being created all the time by different companies. In 2010, the Credit Karma score and a new score by Equifax were introduced. To date, there is little known about how these scores have been tabulated. Equifax has kept their new score secret, which enables them to sell more scores to the general public, since consumers have no way of knowing if the Equifax score is different from the FICO score. Most of these sites withhold the true name of their scores, so consumers can't distinguish between them. In many cases, consumers buy into this lack of transparency and wind up with a score they thought was the one they truly wanted to buy, unaware that it may have a significantly different numerical range.

Besides the scores mentioned previously, there are other scores that directly affect us as consumers. These scores are insurance credit scores.

Although FICO offers credit scores to insurers as a tool for evaluating risk decision making, they are not the same as mortgage credit scores; different factors are taken into consideration in the tabulation process. Besides the insurance scores being different from mortgage scores, there are also various models of insurance scores used by different types of insurance underwriting companies. Since different kinds of insurers might have varied ideas of what causes more risk for their product, they must have a scoring model that takes into consideration factors relating to each offering. There may be a big difference in what information is considered when evaluating risk for issuing life insurance as opposed to homeowner's insurance. In this industry, FICO is not the only company that offers insurance scores used in weighing risk. Large insurance companies, like State Farm, have created their own insurance credit scores that are used in-house.

"While there is a difference between 'credit scores' and 'insurance scores,' there may also be an important difference between insurance scores used for rating one type of insurance versus another type. For instance, the credit attributes and the weighting of those attributes to develop an insurance score for private passenger automobile insurance may be different than a score used for commercial automobile insurance, or for homeowners insurance."[14]

Here are a few types of FICO insurance scores offered and listed on the fico.com site:

○ FICO Insurance Risk Score (auto and property) at TransUnion

○ CPLS (Canadian Property Loss Score) at Equifax in Canada

○ Experian/FICO Insurance Score (auto and property) at Experian (delivered by ChoicePoint)

○ InScore (auto and property) at Equifax[15]

Like mortgage FICO scores, insurance scores are also based on a range that reflects the lower score as the higher-risk individual. The insurance credit score is just one factor taken into consideration in the insurance underwriting process. An insured's age, marital status, geographical location, driving history, and even whether the automobile will be garaged are potential factors that make a difference in premiums. The

---

14   MJ Miller, June 2003, The Relationship of Credit-Based Insurance Scores to Private Passenger Automobile Insurance ... http://www.progressive.com/shop/EPIC_CreditScores.pdf.
15   FICO website, January 2011, http://www.fico.com/en/Products/Scoring/Pages/FICO-Insurance-Risk-Scores.aspx.

Fair Isaac insurance score calculation, as well as the mortgage FICO score, use similar factors that are broken down a bit differently:

Payment history is 40 percent, length of credit history 15 percent, amount of debt 30 percent, new credit 10 percent, types of credit used 5 percent.

Ordering Your Credit Reports
To access your credit report and know your credit score, you need to order them. You have to know what's included when you do so, because when you order your scores and credit reports from online sites, such as in response to advertised annual credit or free credit reports, they are not FICO scores unless they specifically indicate they are FICO. The scores are not free, just the credit reports. In 2010, the US Senate passed a bill to give consumers who were denied funding a free copy of their credit scores. Congress is working to make this the law.

If you would like to review your credit profiles from Experian, TransUnion, and Equifax reports, you can get them all free once each year. If you have been denied financing based on your credit report, you can also get a free copy. Under the Fair Credit Reporting Act, CRAs were legally forced to set up a site to supply you with the free reports. They are available at www.annualcreditreport.com.

When ordering the reports on this site, you must indicate the state you live in and request all three of your reports. You will need to fill out a form that confirms your identity. After filling out this information, you will be directed to a page to check off all the reports you want. As you order each bureau's report, you will be transferred to each of the bureaus individually, and more information will be requested. Once you order one report, you will have to go back to the home page to order the next, until you have all three. These directions are current based on 2011. Don't be confused and think you have to pay for reports. They will do their best to have you take the bait and pay. Even though they have a legal obligation to provide you with your credit reports for free, they are also trying to make money by getting you to order their products and scores. Under all the colorful marketing you will see, in small type, a sentence that says, "Move on to my free report," or something similar. This is where you want to go.

It is very secure to order your reports and scores online at www.annualcreditreport. They go through great efforts to protect your identity and private information. I believe it is easier and more secure to order your reports online than through the mail, as long as you have a firewall on your computer.

Credit reports can also be ordered through mailed request with proof of address and Social Security number. You must provide a copy of your license, utility bill, and some form of proof of a Social Security number (a copy of your card or tax return). It is important that the proof is up to date. You will need to go to the credit bureau sites to get the current addresses. Since they do change, we will not list them here. In your request, list your name, Social Security number, date of birth, and current address. If you have lived there for two years or less, put the previous address as well. Make sure to indicate you would like your free annual credit report.

If you do want to see your scores, you will have to pay for them. When you order scores from online sites other than www.myfico.com, you need to make sure you know what score it is and how it varies from a FICO score (scores a mortgage lender uses). The scores available are PLUS, Vantage, Credit Karma, Equifax, and FICO. Some Equifax products offer the FICO score for one bureau, but they are trying to eliminate these products so that they can sell just their own scores. So be careful.

Remember, many sites offer free credit reports and scores, but there is only one that is legally obligated to give you a free credit report annually: www.annualcreditreport.com.

If any site requests your credit card to supply you with a free credit report, it means they will automatically charge your card if you do not cancel the supposed free offer. Even annual credit report tries to trick you into giving them your credit card. Do not give your card if you truly want a free credit report. Just keep looking at the fine print until you find the free road.

Chapter Three

Shopping for a Mortgage or Loan

Most consumers believe if they have enough money in the bank, are paying their bills on time, and have the right, provable income, they won't have a problem getting financing or refinancing on a property. It is a bit more complicated than that, and many unseen factors may come into play. These factors could drastically change their ability to save hundreds and thousands, if not millions, of dollars over the life of a loan. The FICO score is used by lenders to determine the credit risk of a consumer shopping for a mortgage. Each consumer's FICO score number could represent the difference between a 4.5 percent interest rate and a 10 percent interest rate. Depending on where the score falls, these differences can equal a monetary fortune over the life of a mortgage. Here is an example of how the FICO score can change unexpectedly and the cost incurred:

Jim and his wife are trying to buy a home in New York City and are shopping for a mortgage of $900,000. Jim and his wife, Susan, both have excellent credit scores, Jim with a 745 and Susan at a 742. With these very good scores, they can qualify for the better rates. In 2010, they are quoted an interest rate of 4 percent, which means their monthly payment is about $4,296. Over the life of this thirty-year fixed rate loan, they will pay $1,546,516. This is a great scenario.

Now, suppose Jim and his wife decided to open a joint Bloomingdale's account a few weeks before applying for a loan. Unknown to either of them, opening and closing a credit account could drop scores up to sixty points. The higher the score, the more of a potential drop it will take. Since they have very good scores, the new credit line reduces both of their FICO scores down to around a 700. Now, the rate goes up to 5.5 percent, and the monthly payment jumps to $5,110. The total cost over the thirty-year period is now $1,839,600 for the same $900,000 fixed mortgage. The higher loan rate boosts their monthly payments by over $800 per month, or an increase of $294,084 over the life of the loan. Jim and Susan may be able to pay points to reduce the rate. A point equals 1 percent of the total mortgage and is charged by the lender to applicants to reduce the interest rate at closing. If it is two points, the cost could be $18,000 upfront—just because they opened a charge account. With both these outcomes resulting from opening a new credit account, we can't assume that Jim and Susan would even be approved for this mortgage with the lowered FICO score.

Since such a small mishap could cost a significant penalty, it makes sense to keep scores high by protecting credit. Learning the rules of credit and what prompts these changes is essential when shopping for one of the largest investments a consumer will ever make.

Inquiries

Consumers usually go to more than one bank to compare rates and fees for a loan. Every time a consumer goes to a third party to apply for a loan, car, credit card, or other financing where the grantor needs to evaluate risk level, a consumer credit report is pulled. This credit review is called a *hard inquiry*. This type of view is considered negative, and it could drop scores two to five points. These hard inquiries remain on the credit report for two years. In other words, trying to save money by shopping around for credit can end up making a loan more expensive.

The other type of inquiry is called a *soft inquiry*. This is when the consumer pulls his or her own credit reports and scores, when applying for most insurance products, and when creditors view credit for promotional purposes. These views do not hurt the credit and are not seen when third parties review the reports. The promotional offers do not become a reduction in score until the consumer actually applies for the card, which would cause a new hard inquiry. Consumers can pull their own credit information one hundred times a day, and it will not affect the score.

To understand inquiries, we must learn more about the companies that provide the credit data to the mortgage lender. These small CRAs, which are either owned by the three bureaus or franchised out, supply the lenders with a report containing the information from all three bureaus (Experian, TransUnion, and Equifax) merged into one report. Bankers refer to these smaller CRAs as pulling services, and we will do so as well. There are hundreds of these pulling services that act as third parties between the banker and the credit bureaus. They provide the bank a copy of a consumer's three credit reports merged with three FICO scores. Each bureau's information has a FICO score that represents the risk level associated with it. The pulling service charges the lender a fee for the service.

Information provided by the pulling services to the lender is processed through a FICO score, which helps the lender define the consumer's risk category. There are also different models of each FICO score from which the lender chooses. The different models can vary on how inquiries affect the score.

If a lender pulls a consumer's credit report, the consumer has a legal right to get a copy. But the lender may not be able to provide that copy to the consumer legally. Banks must follow certain privacy policies and abide by laws the banking department regulates. The consumer can ask for the phone number of the pulling service and request a copy directly. The pulling service must provide the consumer with a free copy.

The lender also chooses a period of time, called a *window*, in which to allow consumers the chance to shop for the best rates. During this time—usually fourteen, thirty, or forty-five days—multiple inquiries will affect the score less. Within this period, whether the consumer has one or eighty lenders pulling their credit and causing inquiries, the score can only be impacted as if one lender pulled or inquired into the consumer's credit history.

In my study of inquiries, I spoke with a representative from FICO,[1] and I took information from the FICO site. This is what I learned: "The impact from applying for credit will vary from person to person based on their unique credit histories. In general, credit inquiries have a small impact on one's FICO score. For most people, one additional credit inquiry will take less than five points off their FICO score. For perspective, the full range for FICO scores is 300–850°. Inquiries can have a greater impact if you have few accounts or a short credit history."[16]

After being in the credit restoration and education business for twenty years and reviewing thousands of credit reports, I find this statement to be too general and even false in most cases.

> A middle score is when banks extending credit use the middle number of the three FICO scores representing each credit bureau's information.

Before we get into examples, it is important to define a "middle score." Each of the three credit reports has a FICO score that represents the information on that bureau's report. Each report could vary, so every consumer will have three different scores. If your Experian is a 740,

---

16   My Fico website,2010, http://www.myfico.com/CreditEducation/CreditInquiries.aspx.

TransUnion is a 690, and your Equifax is a 725, the middle score would be a 725.

With that in mind, here are some examples of how inquiries can affect the score.

- John Smith has a middle score of 742 and applies for a mortgage with three lenders over the course of 2.5 months. His score can drop six to twelve points, which could make a substantial difference in his rate or ability to get the loan he wants.

- Andy Stone, who followed the same steps as John Smith, had a middle score of 680 and was applying for an FHA loan. He would be paying higher fees for his loan when his score dropped six to twelve points as well.

The part about having few accounts we all know. If you only have two accounts, your score will most likely be low in the first place, so the inquiries will impact you even more.

FICO went on to explain:

> "Research has indicated that the FICO score is more predictive when it treats loans that commonly involve rate-shopping, such as mortgage, auto and student loans, in a different way. For these types of loans, the FICO score ignores inquiries made in the 30 days prior to scoring. So, if you find a loan within 30 days,

the inquiries won't affect your score while you're rate shopping. In addition, the score looks on your credit report for rate-shopping inquiries older than 30 days. If it finds some, it counts those inquiries that fall in a typical shopping period as just one inquiry when determining your score."[17]

This is where it starts to get confusing, but I did manage to get some more info that might help. When it comes to mortgage inquiries, car inquiries, and student loan inquiries, all these types of inquiries affect the score differently than the rest. Within a thirty-day period, twenty inquiries would only affect a score as much as one inquiry, or two to five points. After the thirty-first day, each inquiry is treated separately and could hit the score by a reduction of two to five points. FICO goes on to say that any grouping of inquiries within thirty days prior to your immediate loan shopping will also be treated as one inquiry. If shopping for a mortgage, student loan, or car in one thirty-day period, each of these categories will be counted separately, so you would have the impact of three inquiries (and perhaps up to six- to fifteen-point deduction). If you had shopped for another car four months prior and had twenty inquiries in a thirty-day period, those would be counted as one inquiry as well. Student loan inquiries are discussed further in chapter 4.

FICO explained why inquiries are viewed negatively: "Large numbers of inquiries also mean greater risk. Statistically, people with six inquiries or more on their credit reports can be up to

17 My FICO website, 2010, http://www.myfico.com/CreditEducation/CreditInquiries.aspx.

eight times more likely to declare bankruptcy than people with no inquiries on their reports."[18]

Pulling Services

Let's return to the pulling services and the companies that use them to order consumers' merged reports. Each lender (of any kind) uses a pulling service to view reports; this view causes an inquiry and affects the score. Since there is so much misinformation about credit and scores, I wanted feedback from the pulling services as well. Since they provide the lenders with the FICO scores used to decide loan interest rates, it is important to see if their information is different.

After speaking with LandAmerica, Kroll Factual Data, Rels, CIS Pulling Service, and Equifax Mortgage Solutions, it seemed I had received a lot of conflicting information. Information from the pulling services did not match with what FICO expressed. The pulling services said scores dropped about two to three points for each inquiry, unless the inquirers were student loan, mortgage, or car lenders and the inquiries were made within the selected window. The big surprise was these pulling services said that after the fourteen-days (what the banks have chosen as the time allotment for windows in 2010), each of the inquiries that were made within that window began to count as a reduction of two to three points. This means that if a consumer shops for a mortgage with twelve lenders within the fourteen-day window, once the window ends, the score could drop thirty-six points.

---

18 My FICO website, education 2010 http://www.myfico.com/crediteducation/creditinquiries.aspx.

After viewing thousands of credit reports and seeing reports before and after inquiries, I can say the information given above is inaccurate. If the information were true, most of the reports I have seen would have a much lower score.

As discussed earlier, the pulling services offer variations of the same score, and lenders pick which one they would like. These variations can change the length of the window of time inquiries affect the scores. In the past (before the economy changed in 2007) lenders were using thirty-day windows and getting ready to change to forty-five-day windows. Since 2009, most lenders have chosen fourteen-day windows due to the more conservative lending attitude. So we now know the windows could vary depending on the scoring model lenders use. This makes it even more confusing but does explain why sometimes inquiries impact the score differently than we expect.

It also became clear that we could not rely on the pulling service to give us valid information. The other issue concerned the pulling services' description of point decreases, which was up to two points lower, per inquiry, than FICO described.

Scoring Examples
Here are some examples of the mortgage FICO score explained by pulling services. They should help clarify this information. Keep in mind each inquiry reduces the score two to three points.

1. A bank picks a model with a fourteen-day window for inquiries. This means if you start shopping for a loan on day 1 (mortgages, car loan or lease, student loan) and the loan closes after seven lenders pull your credit by day 13, your score would drop as if you had only one inquiry. If your score was a 755, it could be a 753 after the fourteen-day window if all those inquiries counted as a two-point reduction.

2. Another bank picks a model with a thirty-day window for inquiries. If you start shopping for a loan on day 1 and ten bankers pull your credit score by day 30, that counts as one inquiry. At days 32 to 50, you have ten more bankers pull your credit score. Your credit is pulled again on day 60 for the bank you want to use to close your loan. If you started at a 755, the score is now a 731. It has dropped twenty-four points (two points for the first ten inquiries within the thirty-day window plus twenty-two points for the eleven inquiries within the last thirty-two to sixty days). If you started at a 689, your score would have dropped to a 665.

> The key to how the pulling services define affects of inquires is after the lender's window expires (depending on the model chosen by lender), each inquiry is counted as a two- to three-point reduction of the score. The score has the potential to decrease dramatically. In my experience, this statement is inaccurate!

3. The last lender picks a model with a forty-five-day window for inquiries. If you start shopping on day 1 and have thirty-five lenders pull your credit within that window and one lender pulls it on day 48, your original 755 score would now be, at the most, a 751 (your first thirty-five inquiries count as two points, and the last inquiry on day 48 reduces the score two points as well). You would lose four points.

The key is after the lenders window expires (depending on the model chosen by lender), each inquiry is counted as a two- to four-point reduction in the score. The score has the potential to decrease dramatically. Once your score falls below 740 and then below 720, your interest rate on the mortgage you are applying for will increase. You become a higher risk. You can also be denied funding if your score decreases further, or if the type of loan you are applying for will not take less than a certain score. Be careful when you shop for a loan, and make sure your timing is right. Keep these rules in mind.

According to myfico.com, FICO scores bought directly on their site are more forgiving. If you shopped for a loan four times in a year and had ten inquiries in four different bundles of thirty-day periods, each bundle would be counted as one inquiry, or a two- to five-point reduction.[19]

Since there is a vast amount of varying information, I decided it would be best to speak directly with a FICO specialist to

---

19   http://www.myfico.com/crediteducation/creditinquiries.aspx, 2010.

get confirmation. The FICO expert told me that the mortgage scores given to lenders by the pulling services follow this same model used by the consumer FICO scores. His description of this score was very different from what the FICO site said. According to him, each thirty-day period of inquiry bundles (for auto and mortgage inquiries only) has no point reduction. He stated that there is also a fifteen-day extension after the thirty-day period, called a "de-duplication period," during which all inquiries count as one inquiry, or a two- to four-point reduction. For example, on days 1 to 30, you have twelve lenders pull your credit score and there would be no point reduction. After the thirty-day period, you have five more lenders pull your credit score within the fifteen-day de-duplication period. During this fifteen-day period, inquiries would only count as one inquiry. Your score would be reduced by two to four points. He did say that depending on the model the lender uses—fourteen, thirty, or forty-five days—the score can vary. When I asked the FICO expert why his definition was so different from the rest, he said, "It is so complicated that most people don't understand it and wind up giving false information and creating misconceptions."

What the expert said was clearly denied by the pulling services that provide the mortgage lenders with scores. The five pulling services I spoke with were adamant about after the window ends, each inquiry is viewed separately, and bundles are not considered for past windows. Each

> The one thing that is very clear is your lender's FICO score can be different from the FICO consumer site score.

inquiry would reduce the scores two to four points after the current window expired. So, if you have twenty-five inquiries after the window expires, your score can go down more than fifty points.

This is quite a bit of conflicting information, and which expert do we believe? The one thing that is very clear is your lender's FICO score can be different from the FICO consumer site score.

Even if the pulling services are wrong about each inquiry counting as a two-point reduction after the window expires, the fact remains that different window models are used. This will alter the consistency of the FICO consumer and FICO mortgage scores. From my experience, FICO consumer and FICO mortgage scores are usually a little different. If FICO uses a thirty-day window and your Mortgage Bank uses a fourteen-day window, there can be a difference. It should be noted that inquires other than mortgage, auto, and student loans will not be viewed in batches and will reduce your score individually two to five points.

To avoid inquiry score reduction when shopping for a mortgage, do not get increases on credit limits, shop for a car, open new credit, or have long periods between bankers pulling your reports. Try to shop for your loan quickly and close on the loan as soon as possible.

What You Need Years Before Getting a Mortgage

Times have changed and continue to change at a rapid pace. In 2006, it seemed the only requirement for a consumer to get a loan was a pulse. In 2009, if you had an excellent FICO score of 740 to 850 and if the required income-to-debt ratio and appraisal came in at the right value, you were ensured the best rates. In 2010 and going into 2011, consumers must become aware of more challenges. Major banks—like Wells Fargo, Bank of America, Chase, and many others—require *open*, *active*, and *seasoned* trade lines to be approved for a loan. No matter how high the income, FICO scores, or the value of the home may be, if the right amount of open and active credit lines are not on your credit profile, you may be denied. With this in mind, it is of great value to begin building your credit two to three years in advance of thinking about getting a new mortgage or refinance.

> Many lenders require you to have *open*, *active*, and *seasoned* trade lines before they will approve a loan.

What does this mean? Active open credit lines are now a requirement for many mortgages. Here is an example.

A consumer has one credit card that has been open and active for six months; one active, new, auto loan; a closed PC Richards and Macy's account; and a closed, one-year-old Bloomingdale's card. This consumer's FICO score is 745. The loan being applied for is over $720,000. This consumer could be denied this mortgage from many banks. Why would this happen? Banks now require more active, open, and seasoned accounts than they did in 2007. Each bank may have a different requirement, so it is important to check well in advance.

Active, Open Accounts

If consumers do not use their revolving credit (all credit that can be maxed out and only minimum payments are required), these accounts become inactive, and grantors can close them if they so choose. Besides closed accounts, scores can drop up to twenty points for inactivity of credit. This means that revolving credit accounts must be used consistently to ensure the best score benefit.

Seasoned Credit

Seasoned credit refers to accounts that have been open for over one or two years. Some mortgages require a combination of one or two active and seasoned accounts that are a year or more old. This same type of loan may also ask for two more accounts that are twenty-four months old. Other loans may require one seasoned and active account. *It is important to speak with your mortgage professional well in advance to determine what the requirement is for the loan you may need!* Requirements vary depending on the amount of the mortgage, and whether it is a conforming, nonconforming, jumbo, or FHA loan.

Another factor to consider when preparing for a loan is the time requirement needed to build good, seasoned credit. When opening credit, your score can be reduced by up to sixty points for a year. This also applies to closing credit. Adding yourself as an authorized user onto a relative's old and excellent credit card account may very well increase your credit score, but it will not be viewed by the bank as *your* credit. You must have the time to establish your open, active accounts before applying for the loan.

If consumers don't give themselves the time they need to build credit well in advance of buying or refinancing a loan or property, it can be very disappointing and costly. Finding a property for sale at well under its real value and not having the credit needed for approval could mean the loss of a great investment opportunity at best. On the other side, it could be losing the chance to save thousands on mortgage payments when applying for a lower interest rate on a current refinance.

The point I am trying to make is contact a mortgage professional now, who can explain all the requirements for the exact loan you may be interested in. Why not learn today what is needed to make an easy successful mortgage approval tomorrow.

Possible Consequences of Paying Off Balances
Since 2009, there have been some interesting reactions from creditors when consumers have paid down revolving debt. Prior to getting a mortgage when buying a home or refinancing, many of us advise our clients to pay down high balances. In 2009–2010, I heard regrets from a few bankers who specialize in mortgage financing and needed an increase of a few extra points in their clients' FICO scores. They came to us seeking advice on what to do after they experienced these events. I remember a client who owned a business and used his American

Express card to juggle expenses while waiting for receivables to arrive. He was trying to take out financing on a $1,000,000.00 plus piece of property he owned outright. He needed twenty points on his score and had a high balance on his card. Paying down his American Express balance to $20,000.00, which was 30 percent of his limit, was the quickest way to reach his goal. The day after he paid down the balance, American Express reduced the limit to $20,000, and we were all surprised and obviously very upset, since his score dropped seventy points. This took him further away from his goal.

In a lot, but not all, of the cases, the clients made very large incomes and had high balances on home equity lines of credit and American Express cards. A few days after reducing balances, American Express or the creditor who issued the revolving line of credit reduced the limit down dramatically, at least 50 percent. This caused the scores to decrease and limited the consumer's purchasing ability.

When consumers pay down debt, the credit profile must be evaluated individually, and if it is a home-equity line or American Express card, there is a higher risk involved. Many home equity lines and Amex cards are necessities for consumers who have them, so the ramifications of this action should be completely understood before consumers pay down debt. Consumers must be aware that creditors are, even with consumers who have never been late, reacting this way, and there is also a possibility their credit lines can be reduced or closed when they pay them down.

Unfortunately, the professionals who helped bring this new credit grantor pattern to light were caught on the frontline of the credit score war and felt the pain of giving advice that backfired. Because of the constant fear and changing reactions to the economic environment, it is more important than ever to learn about new patterns in credit score sensitivities. If consumers have many high balances and a score needs to be boosted promptly, it is important to reduce the revolving credit balance in a methodical way and at the right time.

Credit Profile: A Snapshot

When a lender pulls a credit report and score, they see a view of what has been updated on that consumer's profile at that exact moment. This does not mean they are seeing the actual current status of the individual's credit. Each creditor pays a fee to the bureaus to update information at the time they make the change. Many creditors do not update the reports the moment you pay down a balance, close or open an account, have a late payment, or convince your creditor to remove a negative mark due to their mistake. It is essential to get proof in writing of all changes to your report (especially those pertaining to negative information) prior to applying for a loan. Proof could be a statement (must have your full name, account number, balance to date, and the creditor's information). If it is a letter stating the late payments are being deleted from the account, it must state that clearly besides having the other information described. If you find the report is not a current reflection of your status, you can supply the lender with proof, and they can do a rapid rescore. (A rapid rescore is when the mortgage lender gives the pulling service proof of incorrect information, and the pulling service rescores the credit to reflect the corrected information within seventy-two hours.) If you find your credit is poor and you cannot get proof of changes or would like to improve it, you can call North Shore Advisory, Inc., to see if credit restoration is a viable option. Always check your credit twelve months prior to applying for a loan to make sure it is the best it can be.

Part of preparing for a loan includes understanding what it takes to have the best credit scores. The next chapter is imperative to consumers who would like great credit for any reason but, it will benefit mortgage applicants dramatically.

Chapter Four
Having the Best Credit

Although we know a great deal about how FICO scores work and what affects them, there is much that is kept secret. Every once in a long while, we have come across credit reports in which the consumer has only two to three lines of credit, and the score has been as high as an 800. Usually, having two lines of credit would deliver a low score. How could this be? It is perplexing, but instead of focusing on what we don't understand, we have decided to figure out what, for the most part, ensures great scores.

"Timing is everything," and it definitely rings true for keeping the best scores. Whenever a consumer considers an action that may cause any change in his credit, it must be thought out and taken with all future ramifications in mind. An excellent credit portfolio could be worth thousands of dollars, if not millions.

The following are all insights into how to manage credit while keeping the highest scores in mind.

Great Credit

Having a wide range of credit in your credit portfolio is the most popular and the surest method to build an excellent credit score. We know that the scoring system wants to see who we are as consumers by viewing our payment patterns. The best way for them to see us is by reviewing our ability to manage many types of credit. Revolving, installment, mortgages: these types of credit give the scoring system the ability to predict our risk level.

Revolving credit, as we discussed earlier, includes credit cards, lines of credit, home-equity loans or lines, overdraft on a checking account, store cards, and any account that you decide how much you will charge, up to the limit, and how little you will pay monthly. This type of credit impacts the score the most, because it is the kind over which we have the most control. We can charge as much as our limit allows and pay as little as the minimum suggests. Therefore, when it comes to balances, if they are high on this type of credit, the score plummets downward.

Installment credit (auto loans and leases, student loans) requires the same payment monthly. The balance-to-limit ratio, although it hurts when high, does not impact the score as much as revolving credit. Since consumers don't decide how much they will pay monthly but only if they will pay on time, they are not in

> Having a wide range of credit in your credit portfolio is the most popular and the surest method to build an excellent credit score.

control of making all the decisions. Because of the nature of how the payments are set, this type of credit is not weighted as heavily on the score when it comes to balance-to-limit ratios. Because of this, the score is not decreased as much if balances are higher, as with revolving credit.

Mortgages are in their own category, and the balances affect the score the same way installment loans do. Having too many mortgages hurts the scores, since you are viewed as an investor and, therefore, a higher risk. The only type of mortgage that can cause dramatic dips in the score due to balances are interest-only loans. Since you are not paying principal and, in some cases, barely paying interest on these loans, balances can increase above the initial limits. Once the balance goes above the limit, the score takes a major dip. It could be up to, or in some cases, even over one hundred points. When balances are over the limit, it is like a fire alarm to the score. The score alerts the creditor or lender that the consumer is at major risk for default. Most studies show when a consumer is maxed out on credit accounts, it is a precursor to late payments and a real possibility of no payments.

Mortgages, different lines of credit, overdraft on a checking account, and various types of credit cards indicate consumers' ability to manage credit. But it is important to know that when you build your credit portfolio by opening new accounts, the score will drop until they become seasoned (over a year or two old). So please, do not run out and open credit if you are applying for a loan within the next year. This is only to be done when you will not need to open credit for a year or so.

Keep accounts open, because closing credit, as we discussed earlier, will also hurt the credit score, possibly reducing it up to sixty points for a year or more. When you close credit, you are taking away a valuable view of how you manage your accounts. When the score is less able to view your full ability to manage all types of credit, it causes a drop in your score since your risk level has risen.

Opening credit is also an action that studies show occurs in many cases before a default pattern. If a consumer suddenly starts opening credit accounts, she has the ability to charge more than she can afford, and the likelihood to default increases. If she continues with her limited credit, the risk is lessened. Besides being a higher risk for nonpayment, there is also no history of paying patterns on the account. The account is a newborn, and because of this, the score drops. Every year the account ages, the score starts to increase.

Scores love seasoned credit. The older the better, the higher the score can go, and it doesn't even matter to the score if the account is closed. As long as it is old, it has the potential to increase the score as much as fifty to one hundred points. We have seen accounts at one bureau that were twenty years old. The other two bureaus had the same information, other than that aged account, and the scores were eighty points less. If an aged account is closed, it can be removed after two years by the creditor. This is why it is best to keep all accounts open and active. If you close an old account, it can be removed and cause dramatic dips in the scores. Just because you have many credit cards, it does not mean you have to charge high balances. You can keep a card open and active by charging $10 over a two-month period annually.

If a consumer had no credit and suddenly acquired two to three accounts, this would also be seen as a big risk for default. If you think about it this makes perfect sense. If John were new to the credit system and began opening and managing multiple accounts, the chances he will be delinquent are much greater in the beginning years of learning how to manage this new financial system. Once his credit is over a year or two old, he is much more financially trustworthy.

Closing any and all types of credit that show on the credit profile can reduce the score. As mentioned previously, one of the symptoms of pending defaults is the closing of credit lines. Because studies have shown this pattern occurs before consumers stop paying on credit, the score will immediately drop. The higher the score, the more of a drop will occur when the first account closes. The fewer accounts on the credit profile, the more of an effect it will have when credit closes. When closing any type of credit, it is extremely important to act at the right time. When applying for a loan within a year, it is imperative *not* to close any credit, or the damage to the score can be devastating. There is no way to get seasoned credit in the consumer's name without taking the time to build it. Once credit is closed, there is no turning back without damaging scores.

Paying patterns are a major asset to building the best scores. If you pay on time, your credit will be good. But, if you pay early (ten to twelve days), you may find your scores are as much as fifty points higher. Paying early does boost the score and is a great way to make sure you get the maximum points to ensure the lowest rates and greatest opportunity a score can afford. Many real estate investors who find they have lower scores because of so many mortgages (closed or open) can use this method to hedge against high drops in their FICO.

If a consumer is getting ready to refinance their mortgage and has a 720 score, and if a car lease is expiring, he should extend it a few months so it won't close during the financing process. If the lease isn't extended and the credit is pulled after the last payment, the score could drop fifty points, which would leave this consumer out in the dark. Depending on the size of the mortgage, a loan may be denied or a hefty change in the interest rate may occur. In this case, it would be better to extend the lease an extra few months until the loan closes successfully. This is just one example of many occurrences that may ruin a great opportunity for savings and a better life.

Keeping your credit to yourself is a valuable way to stay in control and maintain the best scores. Once you cosign for a loan, you are putting your credit into someone else's hands. Many consumers want to help out a friend or loved one and don't understand the legal and credit ramifications of cosigning. Not only will the cosigner be subject to the other parties paying patterns showing up on their credit, but if the other party defaults, the cosigner is responsible for the balance due. As my father always said, "The road to hell was paved with good intentions," and we surely know that sometimes mistakes happen and late payments occur. The last thing any of us wants is a drop of sixty to one hundred points in our score. If a relative dropped a bill behind his dresser and didn't make a payment on time and it showed up on our credit profile, we would be livid. It is a great thing to help others, but sometimes consumers go too far.

Joint and Authorized User Accounts

A joint account is when two individuals are equally responsible for credit card payment patterns and debt. When having joint accounts, the two applicants have a legal obligation to whatever debt is on the credit card. Each credit card user can use the card, and whatever paying patterns occur will affect both of their credit profiles equally. If one defaults on the debt owed, the other is still responsible. This can be a problem if one person loses their job and late payments occur; it will ruin both cardholders' credit. If credit is kept separate and one person loses a job, at least the other person's credit can be saved. The couple can decide which individual's credit will be sacrificed and left unpaid until finances change. This can help in refinancing situations. Today, most consumers refinance to lower monthly mortgage payments and make financial obligations less. In this situation, since one of the consumer's credit will still be good, the couple can save money when refinancing if rates are low.

Authorized user accounts are different, since a second individual is placed on a primary cardholder's credit card for the sole purpose of being allowed to charge on the account. Most authorized users are not responsible for the payments but will see the payment pattern on their credit profile. If the authorized user is taken off the credit card, the history, in most cases, can be removed as well. These accounts can dramatically increase or decrease the credit, depending on various factors. The problem with authorized credit is it cannot be used as a valid credit line when a bank is deciding if they will approve a loan. Most mortgage banks will not approve a loan if the consumer does not have a certain number of accounts of their own but has many authorized user accounts.

Maintaining Balances

Balances are a great positive or negative to having high scores. We know revolving credit impacts the score the most when it comes to balances. Keeping revolving credit balances at 10 percent of the limit gives consumers the maximum benefit to the score. Having balances over the limit could

> The older the age of the credit, the better it is for the credit score.

decrease the score as much as one hundred points. As the balances creep higher and higher toward the limit, the further the score drops. Remember: no matter how few or many accounts you have, if your balances are high, your score will drop dramatically.

It may be a great savings for a consumer to transfer balances on credit card debt to a low interest account, but that could also have a large impact on the scores. If your balance is now at your limit but you are saving 10 percent interest on a large debt, it may be great for the short term. If you are looking for financing, however, it could cost much more throughout the life of your new mortgage loan. Again, timing is everything!

Building Credit

Building credit takes at least one to two years, unless you get authorized credit cards through another individual. As I stated earlier, this could be an issue if the primary cardholder defaults or has late payments on the card. That said, having a relative, friend, or spouse put you on his or her account as an authorized user is one way to get instant credit. The older the credit, the better it is for the credit score. If you do decide to take this avenue, make sure the account you become a part of is as old as possible.

Here's a brief summary of things to consider before making this choice:

- Be sure the individual whose account history you are taking has no previous late payments, and they feel confident there will be none in the future.

- Be sure the creditor will not view you as responsible for the debt if the primary cardholder defaults or goes to bankruptcy.

- The primary cardholder must understand that the person now holding the new authorized card has the ability to use his credit at any time, even if the actual card is not provided.

If you do not want to become an authorized cardholder, you must start opening credit on your own. To be approved for credit, you can get secured credit cards or ask your bank (where you have a checking account) if they would issue you a secured credit card. Your bank may be able to offer you a regular credit card as well, but this is done on a case-by-case basis, so there is no guarantee. Try to open two secured credit cards, and use them immediately. Do not charge over 10 percent of the limit, and pay the minimum payment the day you get the bill in the mail rather than on time, without paying the whole account off for six months. This will create activity and great payment history.

Once these cards are open for six months, you can apply for a regular Mastercard/Visa account. Make sure to check online to see which Mastercard/Visa is likely to be approved for someone with limited credit. There are many sites where you can find descriptions of which cards are approved more easily. Do not close any credit for at least three years, since closing credit hurts your score, and that is the opposite of your goal. Be sure you continue to build on each credit card as you acquire more and more credit. I would try to have four to eight credit card accounts. These might include two to three credit cards (Mastercard, Visa, American Express, Discover), two to three store cards, overdraft on a checking account (hard to get, so it should be the last type of credit you apply for). Of course, some installment credit is good as well. This would include car loans or leases and a student loan.

Remember, opening and closing credit hurts your score for one year, so time this event correctly. Don't run out and open or close credit accounts once you establish them if you are applying for a loan within a year.

Changing Your Name
When changing your name, it is imperative that you change everything within a short time. It can be a complicated, tedious process to change your name. If you decide you need to do this, please make sure it is timed to best benefit your current and future financial plans. When it comes to a name change, timing is everything. If you are going for financing within the year, it is best to wait until after you get your loan. Many consumers who change their name prior to getting a mortgage find their credit reports in error, the bank writing the loan requires more documentation, and it adds more stress to an already intense situation.

When you change your name, it is surprising who requests what information. You even have to supply proof of a Social Security number and new name plus a divorce decree (if that's the reason for the name change) to EZ-Pass. It is a great idea to have all your proof in one place, and spend a few hours calling and faxing all your creditors. Here are some of the areas to remember: new Social Security card, credit cards, license, insurance cards, life insurance, health insurance, bank accounts, EZ-Pass, store credit cards, wills, homeowner's policies, automatic bill payments, pet insurance, IRS, car registration, stock accounts, and investment accounts.

Foreigners' Credit, Common First and Last Names, and Similar Names

A common problem we see is the same or similar names among consumers. Sometimes it occurs when they are immigrants from other countries and, in other cases, just a coincidence. I can't tell you how many Mohammed Hossains there are! This is a great problem and instigates so much confusion and mix-ups with CRAs. We had one client who couldn't get a mortgage for eight months because of negative credit that was not his, appearing and reappearing again and again. He eventually changed his name, and that was a whole other overwhelming process in itself.

Joyce Johnson, John Collins, Jack Smith, Juan Rodriguez, Miguel Diaz, Jane Smith, Mohammed Hossain, Ahmed Singh, and there are many more. These are all common names and cause extreme chaos with reporting agencies! If your name is common, always make sure to check your credit six months prior to applying for financing. This will give you the time to make any corrections well in advance.

Consumer Credit and Mistaken Identity

Here you are, proud as can be at the birth of your first child and the decision to name him after your grandfather and yourself: John Laurence Jr. At this moment, I am sure no one is thinking about the ramifications of this sentimental and proud moment on the future of both parties' credit.

Experian, TransUnion, and Equifax pull your credit profile through their computer system by using your name, Social

Security number, and address. This is how they gather information about you. When they go through this process it causes many inaccuracies and problems, since two people with the same name, and who may have lived at the same address, are often confused with each other.

If, down the road, John Smith Jr. has credit issues, John Smith Sr. may wind up with bad credit, and vice versa. It is always at the worst time that this is revealed. Even if we are able to remove this negative information, it usually comes back within a year or so. It is a constant battle to keep each individual's credit separate. For the rest of their lives, they must view their credit at least five to six months before applying for any new credit to correct any false accounts on the reports. Be very careful when naming your child!

Divorce and Credit
After evaluating credit for over twenty years, it is clear that divorce and credit usually equal low scores. Having separate credit accounts, credit cards, car loans and leases, student loans, mortgages, and lines of credit is the smartest course of action when you are married. Unfortunately, having separate mortgages is usually impossible, since most people need both incomes to be approved for a mortgage.

When a divorce is pending, many attorneys advise their clients to stop paying all credit attached to joint accounts. This will destroy both consumers' credit and scores. One new late payment can bring down a credit score one hundred points, so you can imagine what many such payments would do. If you are a joint cardholder or an authorized user, your score can be affected if there are late payments on the credit profile.

If each individual is already the sole responsible party for their credit, new late payments will only hurt them. Even if a spouse pays the wife's or husband's credit card bills, it is not necessary to be a joint credit card holder.

The other problem we find is many divorce attorneys do not protect their clients regarding mortgages. If an individual decides to sign the deed for their home over to their spouse but the mortgage is not refinanced without the non-deed holder's name, what good is it? Ten years down the road, should the homeowner default on the mortgage, the former spouse—who hasn't owned the home in ten years—is still legally responsible for the mortgage. Since the mortgage is still in the non-deed-holder's name, it will show up as a negative account and ruin the individual's credit as well. If the divorce decree states that the spouse keeping the home has a certain amount of time (say twelve months) after the divorce to refinance the loan in his or her name solely, what happens if it isn't refinanced and he or she loses a job and defaults on the payments? We came across this situation recently. The individual wanted to buy a home and couldn't get a mortgage because her score had dropped due to late payments on a mortgage for which she was not supposed to be responsible. She had to go back to the divorce attorney and try to sort it out. Not only was she unable to get the loan she wanted, but she was still responsible to the bank for the unpaid mortgage on the home she had no part of for a decade.

The loan should be refinanced before the divorce is granted if an individual is to be protected adequately.

As you can see, there are ways to increase the possibility of having high credit scores. This also increases your chances of getting credit and getting it at the best possible rate. But no matter how diligent we are at following the suggestions outlined in this chapter, there will likely come a time when we have to deal with negative information on a credit report.

Chapter Five

Negative Information

This is a big topic. Consumers are usually shocked when they find out the real distress negative credit has on credit scores. There are many items that can be considered negative. In this chapter, we will uncover some of the pitfalls that can lead to a reduction in score. Since this book has been written so that each chapter can be studied independently, some of this information has been covered in prior chapters. For those who are reading it from beginning to end, feel free to skip over the duplications.

Lack of Credit

One circumstance that negatively impacts the score is a lack of credit. If a consumer only has one account that is a year old, or no accounts, how can the individual's risk level be evaluated? The answer is poorly. If there is little or no history, the consumer becomes a higher risk, and the score drops. It is important to have many accounts that are seasoned, that is, more than two years old. The older the credit, the more positively it affects the score.

Closing and Opening Credit Accounts
Closing any and all types of credit accounts that appear on the credit profile can reduce the score up to sixty points regardless of who instigates the closing, the credit grantor or consumer. One of the symptoms of future defaults is the closing of credit accounts. Because studies have shown this pattern occurs before consumers stop paying on credit, the score will immediately drop. The higher the score, the larger the drop when the first account closes. The fewer accounts on the credit profile, the more of an effect it will have when credit closes. When closing any type of credit, it is extremely important to act at the right time. It is imperative not to close any credit accounts if you will be applying for a loan within a year; the damage can be devastating to the score. There is no way to get seasoned credit only in the consumer's name without taking the time to build it. Once credit is closed, there is no turning back without damaging scores.

Most consumers don't realize the reaction credit scores have to opening credit. When new accounts are opened, scores can drop up to sixty points and sometimes more, depending on the individual's credit profile. Studies have shown that when a consumer opens many new accounts, the chances of default are greater.

Limit Reductions and Consequences
In 2009, we started to hear about American Express reducing limits or closing credit cards on consumers. American Express was the first creditor to take an aggressive stance to protect

itself from credit card defaults at the consumer's expense. For an example, see chapter 3, "Possible Consequences of Paying Off Balances."

It is important to understand that when the economy went south, creditors were looking for ways to reduce their risk on future defaults. Even if a consumer had no late payments or negative information on the credit profile, if balances are over 50 percent of the limits, it is a red flag for the creditor that the potential to default is there. If you have $50,000 of debt and your limit is $80,000, you can see how a creditor would be thinking of the potential risk in a bad economy. Most creditors wait until balances have been reduced to cut the limit. They are afraid to cut limits when there is a high balance, since the cardholder has a greater incentive to stop paying completely. There are those creditors who reduce the limit, or even close the account, when the balances are high. This can be devastating to the credit score. First, just by closing the account, the score can drop sixty points. Second, by reducing the limit to less than the balance, the score will plummet. When balances are over the limit (even if the balance is $1.00 over), it is a red flag to the scoring systems. The consumer is viewed as a high risk, and the score is driven down dramatically.

We hear the frustration many have when they see their credit limits reduced and credit cards closed despite no history of defaults or late payments. Consumers feel they are being punished for no reason. It is important to keep balances low if you want to protect your limits from decreasing. Keeping balances at no more than 30 percent of limits on revolving credit will keep the creditors at bay in terms of reducing limits.

Opting Out of Credit Cards

In 2010, credit card companies informed cardholders their interest rate will increase, an annual fee will be assessed, or both of these changes will occur. Many people have received letters giving them an option to "opt out" or to continue paying the current rate on an open balance until it is paid in full. The card is then closed, and no future charges can be made.

If the consumer accepts the new, higher, interest rate, the card will stay active. This puts the consumer between a rock and a hard place. If the interest is raised and the balance is high, the cost could be significant. In this situation, my advice would be to pay off the balance (if possible) and keep the card active to help the credit score. Consumers could always charge a small amount of money once a year and pay it off, just to keep the card from closing. The card should not be closed because the consumer might be mad the creditor is giving them an ultimatum. The health of the credit must come first, unless there is financial difficulty.

Though a consumer's first instinct might be to opt out of the card and take a lower interest rate on the balance due, that action will decrease the score. I know this doesn't seem logical. Consumers think if they pay off the balance at a lower rate for five years, they will save money, which makes this the smarter choice. But there are consequences that may cost them more money in the future.

With the credit card rules that went into effect in February 2010, when the consumer chooses the opt-out option, the score will drop up to sixty points. Opting out means the card will close, whether or not there is a balance. *The closing of the account is what damages the credit score.* Besides the sixty-point loss, a line of revolving credit will be lost. The credit score will be affected for at least a year. If the consumer has minimal credit to begin with, the credit score could be hurt indefinitely. We are not accustomed to viewing credit as an investment portfolio, but that is exactly what cardholders need to do. Prior to closing any accounts, the balance of the entire portfolio should be considered.

There are other consequences of opting out of a credit card. You need to consider when the balance will have to be paid. The new rules demand it be paid in no more than five years. For example, if a consumer owes $10,000 and they opt out, the minimum payment will automatically be recalculated and spread out over the five-year period. The consumer must be ready to pay a higher minimum payment, if necessary. Therefore, it is important to think through all of these ramifications before taking the plunge and opting out. There could be more negatives than positives in opting out or closing a credit card.

So remember, once a credit card is closed, whether by opting out or just closing the account, the credit score is going to drop. If the credit card is reopened or a new card is applied for, the score will drop even further. Opening new credit reduces the score up to sixty points as well.

Late Payments

Usually, the thought is if it is just one late payment on a small amount, it won't do much damage. Nothing could be farther from the truth! It doesn't matter if you have a foreclosure or a late payment in terms of your FICO credit scores; it can drop your score up to one hundred points or more. Anything newly negative has a dramatic drop to the score. The higher your credit score, the lower it will drop on your first negative account. Here are two examples.

Case Study: Julie

Her score was an 809, and she had many credit cards, a mortgage and home equity line of credit, car loan, student loan, and a few store cards. Most of these accounts were more than ten years old. She had been excellent at managing her credit, but one July, her American Express bill fell behind her counter, where she left her mail. A month and a half later, she was cleaning and found the bill. It was too late: she was over thirty days late. Of course, she immediately called and paid the bill, but at that point, the late payment was already on her credit report, and her score dropped to a 709. No matter what she said to American Express, they would not remove the late payment notation.

> ### Case Study: Jonathan
>
> His score was a 660, and he had a few accounts on his credit profile. He has a Visa card, Sears card, and a car loan. He had a late payment two years ago on his car loan. His credit was under three years of age. He forgot to pay his Sears bill, and his score dropped to a 625. Since his score was not extremely high and he already had a late payment within the past two years, the score did not drop as much.

The reason the score drops so much when it is high is because once someone has negative information on a credit report, the chances they will default on financing increase dramatically. This is what statistics have shown at FICO. The first hit has to reflect this chance of default for FICO to alarm the lender to the risk involved in approving financing. It may seem wrong to reduce scores so dramatically when a consumer has been managing her credit responsibly for twenty years. FICO has created a new scoring system that will not cause such drops when considering one new late payment or a small collection account (under a $100) on a consumer's credit report. This new score is not being used at this time. Once the economy tanked, it was put aside, since lenders became stricter in their underwriting requirements and did not want to loosen up on any of their risk considerations. The new scores may, however, be used in the next two or three years, depending on the economy.

The other fallacy is if a consumer pays off a debt that was late and becomes current, the late payment will come off the credit report immediately. Or, it will only hurt the score for a short period of time. The truth is the one late payment will stay on the credit for seven years and affect the score for the first six years. Each year after the first, the score will increase, but the damages will be there for at least six years, diminishing as the negative information ages.

Late Fees
We often hear when a late payment shows up on the credit profile, "But I called the creditor, and they told me they would waive the late fee." Well, that is all well and good, but waiving a late fee does not give any indication that the creditor is removing the late payment from your credit report. The late fee, which could be $25.00, is nothing compared to the interest payments you might pay due to the late payment that fee represents. The score drop from that new late payment could reduce your score up to one hundred points and cost you 2 percent or more in interest on a mortgage. I would rather pay ten times the amount of the late fee, as long as the late payment is removed from my credit profile. If a creditor agrees to remove the late payment on the credit profile it is best to get that in writing. This proof could be the difference between great credit and poor credit. Once a consumer has a document in writing, it can always be sent to the CRAs for correction. If it ever reappears on the report, the original letter must be provided to the reporting agencies as proof. If the letter is very old, the creditor may have to provide you with a new one after you explain that the negative reappeared on the report. As long as you keep the original letter in your records, there should be no problem having it corrected. If you speak to a representative from the creditor, make sure to document everything said

in case you don't get the letter the representative states they are sending. Be aware that a late fee and a late payment are completely different things. One is just a one-time fee, and the other could be a four- to five-year process of having low or lowered scores.

Collection Accounts

Collections occur when a consumer owes a sum of money to any creditor and has not paid at all for a long period of time. The consumer has defaulted on the debt, and it is considered uncollectable by the initial creditor. This could be a dentist, doctor, library, credit card, child support, or store debt. One of the most common is AT&T, and we see these collections all the time. Timeshares are also another popular collection.

After a period of time that the debt has been owed and the original creditor has had no luck in collecting the debt, they either sell it for a discounted price to a collection agency or they lend it to a collection agency for a specified period. If within the designated time the agency is successful in collecting the funds, they receive commission. If the collection agency has four months to collect the debt, they become very aggressive, especially as the four months ends, since they want that commission. Many consumers are shocked at the persistency and harassment they get from these collectors. Once they understand the way in which these agencies receive their fees, they have a better understanding of how it works.

The original creditor can lend the debt to four different collection agencies over a period of time So, in reality, a consumer can have five negative accounts, spanning over a five-year period, for the same $100 debt. Each agency can list the same debt separately, updating it each year as it gets passed around and causing a score to keep dropping over and over for the same original account. This can wreak havoc on a credit score and cost hundreds of thousands in interest over the life of a mortgage. This new account (even though it is the same original debt) recurs every year, showing up as a new account, and reduces the score. Since the score drop causes the lender to increase the interest rate to cover their risk of lending money to this low-score consumer, the cost of their loan is much higher. Collections remain on the credit profile for seven years. The score drops the most the first year, and as the collection ages, the score increases. The score is affected negatively for around five years.

Case Study: Sally

Sally has gone to a surgeon for a knee issue, and the receptionist collects $50.00 co-pay for her office visit. The funds are collected in cash, and Sally waives the receipt; she doesn't want it lying at the bottom of her handbag, along with all the other garbage she collects. She tells the receptionist to update it in the computer right away, so she doesn't have to bother with the receipt. The receptionist is very nice, and they have a short, friendly chit-chat, and Sally leaves the office. A few months later, Sally gets a notice that she owes $50.00 to the doctor for the office visit, which she clearly remembers paying for in cash. She calls the office, and no one remembers her paying in cash. The receptionist asks her to send them a copy of the receipt she collected when paying in cash. Sally tells the receptionist exactly what happened the day she paid. The receptionist tells her they hear many stories, but without a receipt, they cannot waive the fee and take it off their books. Sally is very angry and decides she will not pay the $50.00, because it is unfair. She is adamant about it and goes on her merry way. After months and months of bill after bill from her doctor, the office finally sells the $50.00 debt to a collection agency for $30.00. The collection agency starts harassing Sally and tells her they will settle the account for $40.00, if she makes payment immediately. Sally says no and begins to ignore their calls. After a year, the collection agency sells the debt to another collection agency for $20.00. The process continues, as Sally ignores the new company as well. Within a few years, Sally decides to buy a home and applies for a mortgage. The banker pulls her credit and discovers her score is a 610, and she has four collection accounts, one being as recent as three months old, and the others ranging over the past two and one-half years. Sally is furious. The $50.00 debt has now cost her 2 percent in interest on her mortgage. She could have had a loan with 5 percent interest, and now, if she can even afford it, she will pay 7 percent interest since her scores are so low. It could be the difference between a $2,000 a month payment on a $500,000 loan to a $3,500 a month payment on a $500,000 loan. That is a lot of money to pay for a $50.00 debt she already paid. In this economy, she might not even qualify for the loan. Is it worth it to ignore such a minor debt? You decide.

Charge-Offs

Charge-offs happen when a creditor writes off the debt as a loss against profits. This step usually occurs with larger creditors prior to an account going to collection. For example, Ted has a $30,000 debt with Chase, and he was laid off five months ago. Instead of continuing to pay Chase, he opts to pay his mortgage with his savings. Chase calls and calls and cannot get a payment from Ted. Chase charges off the debt as a loss and sends it to a collection agency. This does not mean Ted no longer owes Chase the money, it just means Chase wrote it off as a loss against profits. Many consumers mistakenly believe that once the account is in a charge-off status, they are no longer obligated to pay it. Charge-offs remain on the credit report for seven years, and if it goes to judgment, the judgment will remain on the credit report for seven years from the date it is placed.

Judgments

When a debt goes to collection and the creditor or collection agency decides they cannot collect from a consumer, there can be a lawsuit. Once the creditor serves the consumer and a court date is set, if the consumer does not show up in court (this is usually what happens), the creditor then has a judgment against the debtor. Judgments are enforceable for over twenty years, and although they only stay on the credit report for seven years, they can still stop a consumer from getting a loan. When applying for a mortgage, a lender will have a title report run to see if there are any liens or judgments against the potential borrower. If they find a lien, even though it does not show on the credit report after seven years, it will stop the loan from being approved or delay it at best. An exception to this rule is if a judgment or lien is placed for over $150,000: it can remain on the credit profile indefinitely. Judgments, if recently placed, could drop the score up to one hundred points. The higher the score, the more it drops. If the score was above an 800, it will drop one hundred points at least. As the score gets lower, the drop is less.

Settled for Less than Full Balance
When collections and charge-offs are eventually paid but for a lower dollar amount than originally owed (or the current debt with late fees accumulated), the account is listed as "settled for less than full balance" or simply "settled." In either of these cases, the account is still on the report and still considered a negative account. It will remain for seven years, like most negative info.

Once an account is settled and paid, it will not necessarily change the score. There is only one exception of the score changing with payment. When lenders pull merged reports, as discussed previously, they merge all three bureaus into one report that comes in various formats. Besides the consumer and lender formats differing, each pulling service has different formats for merged credit reports. Many lenders (banks) have formats that show limits for judgments, liens, and all other credit on the report. If a limit is shown that is the same as the balance, it will increase the score tabulated by that lender's pulling service if the balance changes to paid. As discussed earlier, if the balance-to-limit ratio changes, the score will change as well. So if a judgment or lien is showing a $2,000 limit and a $2,000 balance, it will change the score when it is paid and updated. The score will increase.

Settled for Full Balance

When consumers are negotiating a debt, or if a debt settlement company is working to reduce debt, they can get the creditor to report the debt as "settled for full balance" (which means there was no discount to the debt, and the debtor paid it in full) or "settled for less than full balance," which was discussed earlier. Either mark to the credit report does not make any difference at all to the score. The item is still a negative account, and the score is still affected exactly the same. The scores will reduce dramatically. Many consumers are told by collection agencies or creditors that it is better to pay the item in full so that the report shows the account was settled for full balance. I do not know why they say this, other than wanting to collect the full amount of the debt, since the score will reduce the same way in both cases.

Repossessions or Voluntary Repossessions

When a consumer stops paying for their car loan or lease, the car is eventually taken back by the lender or leaser. Once the car is taken back, it is listed on the credit report as a repossession. If a lessee or borrower of a car loan voluntarily gives the car back due to lack of funds, or just no longer wants the car, the effect on the credit and score is exactly the same. The score will drop up to one hundred points, depending on the score prior to the repossession.

Bankruptcy

This discussion is about how bankruptcy affects credit. If you would like to know the specifics of bankruptcy in regards to a personal situation, please contact a bankruptcy attorney in your area. Different states have different rules when it comes to bankruptcies.

The public record of the filing and discharge of personal bankruptcies stays on credit reports for ten years. Most consumers get confused and think filing for bankruptcy means all their debt will be washed off the credit report and only the public record will show on their reports. This is a misconception. In fact, each account included in the bankruptcy stays on the reports for seven years. Each creditor included in the bankruptcy is supposed to update the credit reports that the account is included in the bankruptcy. It is quite rare that all the creditors update each account in either of these cases. Once the account is included in Chapter 7, the creditor knows they will not be paid on the debt. In the case of a Chapter 13, the creditor knows they will be paid a minimal amount of the debt. Updating the credit profiles costs money for the creditor, and at that point, it seems they are not very concerned with the updates. We often see credit reports where the consumer filed a Chapter 7 years ago, and each creditor comes up on the credit profile as a charge-off. Even though the account was included in the bankruptcy, it was never updated. This decreases the credit score and makes it look like the consumer never paid the accounts and did not include them in the filing of the bankruptcy. The score usually comes up much lower than it would if it were updated correctly. A bankruptcy reduces the score dramatically, but by the time a person files bankruptcy, the score is already low, because in the majority of cases, the person has numerous accounts with late payments and may have many charge-offs and collections as well. By the time they get to the actual filing, the scores are already very low.

If a consumer wants to correct the false status of these accounts, they can send their bankruptcy papers to the bureaus and ask for each account to be updated correctly.

Short Sales (SS) and Credit Scores

A short sale is when a bank agrees to take less than the current mortgage owed as full settlement on the loan. With the economy in distress and mortgage defaults at a record high, short sales have been an option with many questions and much concern.

Short sales are viewed by the scoring system as settlements. The reason they are viewed this way is because they are debts that have been negotiated down to a smaller percentage of what was originally owed. If a home originally was worth $800,000 and the homeowner could no longer afford the monthly mortgage payment but had a buyer who would pay $500,000 for the home, it would be presented to the lender. If the lender agreed to waive the additional $300,000 owed on the mortgage, the buyer would close on the property, and the original owner would be released of any obligation to the bank for the lost $300,000. This is the same as negotiating a $30,000 credit card debt down to $10,000. Once the creditor accepts this dollar amount as full payment on the account and the consumer pays, it becomes a settled account. When it comes to the FICO scores, the truth is a short sale is just as bad as a foreclosure in terms of your credit score. Here is what FICO says:

> The common alternatives to foreclosure, such as short sales, and deeds-in-lieu of foreclosure are all 'not paid as agreed' accounts, and considered the same by your FICO® score. This is not to say that these may not be better options for you from a financial perspective, just that they will be considered no better or worse for your FICO score. If you are considering bankruptcy as an alternative to foreclosure, that may have a greater impact to your FICO score. While a foreclosure is a single account that you default on, declaring bankruptcy has the opportunity to affect multiple accounts and therefore has potential to have a greater negative impact on your FICO score.[20]

The information I have gathered from FICO states that the higher your credit score, the greater the drop. It doesn't matter if you have a foreclosure, a short sale, or a settlement, the score will see it as the same negative impact. It should be clear that a short sale is listed on the credit report as a "settled for less than full balance" or "settlement accepted" and there will be no mention of short sale.

---

20 My FICO website, October 2010, http://www.myfico.com/crediteducation/questions/foreclosure-alternatives-fico-score.aspx.

Your score could drop from eighty to one hundred fifty points. If there were late payments prior to the settlement, it could drop an additional sixty to eighty points. FICO states that the higher your score before the delinquency, the lower it will drop when the settlement is updated.[21] There may be exceptions to this rule in rare cases where the bank agrees not to update the credit report as a negative account. The chances of this happening with a short sale are slim, about as likely as with a credit card settlement, and that is about 5 percent of the time.

There are variables other than short sale that impact the credit as well. Is the consumer late on other accounts? If there are late payments on revolving credit (credit cards and lines of credit), installment loans (student and cars), or other mortgages (multiple mortgages), the score could decrease even more. How much credit does the consumer have? If they only have one credit card and a mortgage, it could reflect differently than someone with ten to fifteen good accounts. It is hard to say exactly how much a score will drop for each person who has the same negative information. Every credit report is different, since every credit profile is unique to the individual it represents. But the facts are clear: losing your home will cause the score to drop significantly, and it is not a good thing for your FICO scores.

When it comes to getting a mortgage in the future, there is a difference in going to foreclosure or a short sale. This should be discussed with your mortgage professional. You may have

21 My FICO website, October 2010, http://www.myfico.com/crediteducation/questions.

to wait longer from the date of a foreclosure to be approved, depending on the type of loan.

Tax Ramifications When considering any financial choices where debt is forgiven, it is best to speak with your CPA to discuss what the tax ramifications may be.

Foreclosures

When a consumer stops paying a mortgage and the lender eventually takes over the property, it goes into foreclosure. Just like bankruptcy, most consumers facing this predicament have many late payments, charge-offs, and collections prior to the foreclosure. Therefore, the credit scores are low already. In foreclosure, the scores really can't be very high prior to the actual public filing of the foreclosure, since a consumer must be late for a very long time before the property goes back to the bank. This means the late payments have already reduced the score dramatically. With so many late payments, a score would wind up around a 550 to 620 prior to the foreclosure. It would probably drop sixty points after the foreclosure. Foreclosures remain on the credit report for seven years. If you have a foreclosure, you must wait for a time before a lender will approve you for another mortgage. The time period can fluctuate, so if you are interested in finding out the present rules, speak with a mortgage professional.

Tax Liens

When a debt is owed to the government, a tax lien is usually placed immediately on the debtor and listed on the credit report. This may happen before the consumer even knows they owe taxes. It is amazing how fast the government updates the credit report with tax liens. Uncle Sam wants your money and will make sure you have no way to sell a home or borrow more money unless you fall into the new 2011 regulation. Those eligible are debtors owing under $25,000 and can pay in full, or enter into a payment plan ending in payment in full. The new rule allows these payers's to get the lien withdrawn only if they request the withdrawal letter in advance of payment or setting up a payment plan. Please speak with a CPA before paying a tax lien. Even if you have negotiated a settlement via payment plan with the government and you have paid half the debt you owed, you will still see the original lien with the full, original debt showing open on the report. The lien will not be updated to the current balance until the total settled balance is paid. Once the total is paid, the lien should be updated as satisfied or released. If a tax lien is paid in full consumers can request a withdrawal letter in advance and the lien should be removed. Just because you pay a lien does not mean it automatically comes off your credit profile. In many cases, consumers think once they pay the tax lien or judgment it will be removed. No, no, and no, it will not. In some cases, the government doesn't even update the lien as paid. It is always important to get proof of payment in the form of a satisfaction for judgments and liens. If the creditor doesn't do its job updating the credit profile, the consumer can always use their satisfaction to have it marked paid or released by sending it to the CRAs. Tax liens that do not fall into the 2011 exception remain on the credit report for seven years, and if they are not paid, they will show up on a title search.

Many Mortgages

Of course, a mortgage with late payments is bad for the credit score, but having many mortgages that have always been current is also a hindrance to high scores. The more mortgages a person has, the more negative affect it has on the credit scores. Even if a mortgage is paid, closed, and never had a late payment it still has an adverse affect on the scores if it is one of many. Having more than three mortgages could reduce the scores dramatically.

There are usually two reasons why consumers have many mortgages. The first is repeatedly refinancing a loan to cash out. Cash out means taking money out of the value of the home to use for any purpose, usually to pay debt. If a consumer is repeatedly going through this process, it is an alarm to the score that there is a great potential to default on loans or credit cards. Most people who do this are consistently in debt. This is why the impact to the score is negative: it is a warning that this consumer is a high risk.

The second reason is investment. Investors normally flip homes and have numerous mortgages. A consumer who is an investor is a greater risk than the average homebuyer. As we all know, many investors got stuck with properties that have a lower value than the mortgage debt owed to the bank. In many cases, the investor has to do a short sale and sell their property for less than the value of the mortgage. Because of this, banks have to take losses on the difference between what the mortgage was originally worth and the current value of the property. Some investors couldn't even sell and just let the properties go into foreclosure. You can see why an investor is a greater risk to a lender. This is why having many mortgages reduces the score.

Loan Modification
Several professionals have asked me about loan modifications and how they affect the credit scores. As usual, there is much contradictory information.

A loan modification is when a bank modifies an existing loan made by a lender in response to a borrower's long-term inability to repay the loan. Most loan modifications involve a reduction in the interest rate on the loan, an extension of the length of the term of the loan, a different type of loan, or a combination of these choices. Lenders are open to loan modifications, because they will cost them less than the alternatives.

According to FICO, the scores will not be affected much if the loan has the same original account number. The balance, terms duration (length of time mortgage is paid for), and monthly payment amount will change based on the new information agreed upon by the bank. In the case of a totally new account and loan, the score will decrease. As we know, closing and opening credit can reduce scores as much as sixty points. So, if a new loan is reported and the old loan is closed, the scores will take a big hit for at least a year. The site mentions nothing about partial payment plans. From what I have studied, I believe they are discussing loan modifications that are not part of the government's Making Home Affordable Plan.[22]

---

22   My FICO website, September 2010, http://www.myfico.com/crediteducation/questions/refinancing_

According to the FICO forums where loan modifications are discussed and responses managed by a FICO expert moderator, it is acknowledged that a partial payment agreement will be updated on the credit reports and reduce scores dramatically. These responses are directly related to the Making Home Affordable Plan. These are government-owned loans, and not all loan modifications fall into this category.

According to the Consumer Data Industry Association (CDIA), the loan modification candidate must make partial payments on the loan for a trial period of three months or more, depending on the situation. To qualify for the government's Making Home Affordable Plan, the three months are required for acceptance into the modification program. Since the loan is not being paid as it was originally agreed on, the credit bureau will update it as, "partial payment plan," or, "modified payment agreement," which is a negative to the scores. It could drop the score as much as one hundred points, depending on the individual's overall credit profile. We often see this when consumers go into debt consolidation programs. These programs are given by nonprofit organizations that work directly with the creditors to reduce interest rates on debt and increase the length of time debt can be paid off by consumers. They mark the credit report under each account, "debt consolidation repayment plan," or, "in debt consolidation payment plan." Even though these accounts may have never been late, they are still considered derogatory if they are in a partial payment plan. It does make sense if you think about it. You are now paying back the debt but not at the original terms. Remember, as always, the higher your score is before you have a delinquency, the greater it drops when the new update is reported by the bureaus. The partial-payment-plan mark is considered derogatory, and the score will plummet.[23]

Here is what the CDIC said exactly:

> Mortgage Loan Modification Program—Freddie Mac and Fannie Mae
>
> Freddie Mac & Fannie Mae are offering a streamlined modification program starting 12/15/2008 for a targeted group of borrowers with certain loan criteria. As it relates to credit reporting, all eligible loans under this program must be at least 3 payments delinquent. The consumer must first make 3 payments (reduced payments) during the 3-month trial period before the loan modification will be made effective. During that time, the data furnisher should report the true Account Status Code, which is delinquent, and Special Comment AC (Paying under a partial payment agreement).[24]

My interpretation after reading through much of the CDIC info: it seems that the three trial payments are the three late payments they discuss that are required

---

[23] Consumer Data Industry, December 2008, http://cdia.files.cms-plus.com/Metro2/MortgageLoanModificationProgram.pdf.
[24] September 2010, CDIA site, http://www.cdiaonline.org.

and reported as delinquent. You don't have to be late three times prior to the three trial payments.[25]

To summarize the studies we have found, if you go into a loan modification through the Making Home Affordable Plan, you will most likely have a great decrease in your credit scores. There are times that banks just make mistakes and don't update to the credit bureaus. If this happens, consider yourself lucky in at least one aspect of the situation. If you go through a loan modification with a bank that is not a part of the Making Home Affordable Plan, your credit will reflect the way My FICO defined the credit update. As long as it is the same loan and account number, you will see minor or no change in the credit score.

Student Loans

These loans are a nightmare if you are late. Even students who are in deferment payment plans may see a late payment showing up on the credit profile when they were never late.

Student loans can have a devastating effect on credit scores. Many credit reports show seven or more student loans listed individually for *both* the student and the parents who signed for the loans. Most consumers don't realize that each semester they apply for more loans to pay for school, their credit report reflects the new funds as a completely separate account. By the end of a student's school career, they could wind up with ten to twenty separate loans on their credit profile. What becomes

---

[25] September 2010, CDIA site, http://www.cdiaonline.org.

even worse for the score is if they are late on payments. When it comes to late payments, the reality is these individual credit lines for separate student loans all reflect the same payment history. So, when there is one late payment, it can show on twenty different accounts as if they were all separate late payments. This is a big problem in terms of the score, and we find it very difficult to remove these negative accounts through credit repair.

Students and any consumer responsible for paying back the loan should always confirm with a student-loan representative prior to application how the credit score is affected. All conversations should be documented so that they can be used at a later date if damage occurs from late payments reported after a deferment begins. With the proper information, it can be easier to motivate the student loan credit department to remove erroneous late payments.

We have found cosigning parents and students are both shocked when they have found late payments and sometimes defaults on both of their credit profiles. If a consumer is going to have damage to their report and score if payments are late, they must be in control of making those payments. No one not actually paying the bills can control another person and ensure that all payments will be made. Any person can have the best of intentions, and yet, the damage is done if a mistake occurs or a parent loses a job and cannot make the payment on time. In all situations, having control of making the payments is the only way to ensure they will be paid promptly so that credit profiles will be spared dramatic score drops.

Child Support
Child support payments, whether made on time or not, are usually viewed as negative. Many times, it shows up as a collection or with late payments when there were none. It is hard to get the government to correct any errors on the credit profile. It seems they just don't want to take responsibility for mistakes. This is one of the reasons companies like mine exist (credit restoration).

Joint Accounts
In most cases, if possible, it is best to keep separate accounts as was discussed in the chapter 4. There is a big downside to joint accounts. First, if there is financial stress and no way to make payments on time, both parties will have scars on the credit and sacrifice both individuals' credit scores. If there are not joint accounts, one person's credit can be sacrificed while the other's protected. This strategy ensures there will be a way to lease cars, charge for items needed, and even pay a mortgage or rent on credit. It could make a stressful situation a little easier.

Another downside to a joint account is divorce. Most of us know that when a divorce is in process, the first thing that gets ignored is payments to creditors. This is devastating to the credit score and to both individuals. If there is little combined credit, there is less credit mess with which to deal.

Cosigning

Cosigning is similar to joint accounts in terms of the way it reports on the credit profile. All accounts that you cosign for share the positive and negative information reported to the agencies. Of course, that isn't the case if the item is not listed on your report, since some creditors do not list items on credit. For some, cosigning is a disaster. These situations often occur with mortgages, car leases or loans, and student loans. One group likely to experience difficulties with cosigning is Latin American consumers. They are usually extremely nice to their relatives and friends, so much so that they wind up signing for many accounts without understanding the responsibility and ultimate damage that can be caused. Juan wants to buy a home and does not have enough income, on paper, to get approved by the bank for a mortgage. His mother, Anita, has few expenses and makes a large salary as a tenured teacher in the New York area. Anita agrees to help out by using her good credit and large income as part of the application for the bank loan. Juan buys the house, with every intention of paying on time and keeping the home. The economy goes under, and Juan loses his job as a waiter in a high-end Manhattan restaurant due to very little business. He now cannot afford to pay his mortgage and is embarrassed to ask his mom to help him again. Without realizing it, when he is late on his mortgage payments, his mother's credit score plummets by eighty points. Her 750 score becomes a 670, and as he continues to make more late payments, the score decreases even further. Anita decides to sell her car, which is completely loan free, and buy a brand new Acura. She wants to take out a loan for half of the list price of the car. She sits down with the car salesman, and he pulls her credit. With much surprise and shock, she finds out they will give her a loan but at a very high interest rate. The payment she thought would be $400 a month is now being quoted at $850. As she does a little research after ordering her report, she learns her son can no longer carry the mortgage payment. Not only is her credit ruined, she is legally responsible for the mortgage. This is a complete nightmare.

Another example is George, the landlord. George is in his late sixties and semi-retired. He sold a business about ten years ago and now manages some properties he owns and leases. Interest rates are low, and he decides he can save a small fortune by refinancing some of his mortgages on the investment properties he owns. A few years back, his adult son had asked him to cosign a loan on a car lease. His son had gone through a bad divorce, and his credit was ruined because of it. He had trouble getting a loan for a car, and turning to his father was the best avenue for him. George was more than happy to help after watching his son go through so much mental and financial trauma during the divorce. This was a great opportunity for him to make his son's life a little easier.

When he wanted to refinance his mortgages, George had his banker pull his credit scores and filled out the application for the loan. To George's surprise, he had two late payments on his report from the car loan a few months back. George's score had dropped to a 620 from a 720, and he was unable to refinance any of the mortgages. His son had been out of town five times during that two-month period on business trips and forgot to make his car payments on time. The two late payments cost

George hundreds of thousands over the life of his loan. He would have saved $2,500 a month at the new, lower interest rate if he had been able to refinance all his loans. This was devastating for George and his son. George did decide to have his son send him the monthly payment and he would write out the check to ensure his credit would not be harmed again. Cosigning is risky business on many levels. Be very careful before jumping into it, unless you understand all the pitfalls.

Once you understand what negatively impacts credit scores, it becomes much easier to manage credit with high scores as the goal. Timing is also a big factor in keeping credit great and getting the lowest rates on mortgages, credit cards, and any type of financing.

When late payments and defaults are inevitable because of financial stress, worrying about protecting credit may not be one's first priority. In this economy, many good people wind up hurting themselves more than necessary by worrying too much about their credit, when they should be more concerned with keeping food on the table and a roof over their heads.

Chapter Six

Examples of Financial Stress

In the past few years, consumers and financial professionals (bankers, CPAs, real estate agents, attorneys, and wealth management companies) have asked for clarification about the choices available to people suffering economic hardships. Of course, they want the most practical solution for every situation. Although we deal with many extremely talented and knowledgeable professionals, in this constantly changing mortgage and finance economy, it is hard for many to keep up with available choices. Staying abreast of the rules and options within their own industry is a lot. To then have to be an expert in other areas that affect their clients and prospects is just too much. Since we are on the frontline of financial and credit problems, we come across solutions and options more readily.

Many of these items were discussed previously, and some new items will be defined as well, but following are examples of when some of the choices we defined earlier can be used. All these choices are great if the situation is fitting. It is very important to get as much education as possible before taking action. The wrong choice could have devastating consequences and waste much-needed money for a person already suffering hardship. I will avoid giving too much detail to keep the confidentiality of each individual.

Bankruptcy and Short Sale Example
A woman in her forties lives in New York and owns a home in Florida. She was not able to get any income from her Florida property for various reasons. She was renting in New York and working two or three jobs to cover the costs. Her income was about $38,000. Her Florida home was worth 40 percent less than her mortgage. She owed $50,000 in credit card debt, and she was in and out of the hospital with various medical problems. She was very emotional (as most are about changing their situation). Time and again, we have seen good people try to stay above water for way too long. They wind up paying tens of thousands of dollars more than necessary because they are afraid of the word "bankruptcy." The reason she came to us was to clean up her credit so that she could get better interest rates on her credit card debt and maybe refinance her home. Her credit was a mess, with many late payments on her accounts, charge-offs, and collections.

Here is what she wanted:

Credit restoration is a service offered by many, including my company. Credit restoration companies are hired to dispute and negotiate negative information off the credit reports. Essentially, it is a cleaning of a consumer credit profile. There are laws that apply to creditors, consumers, credit bureaus, and courts. These laws, the Fair Credit Reporting Act, must be upheld for information to be kept on the credit profile. When shopping for this type of company, consumers must be careful. There are many unscrupulous companies out there, trying to cash in at a time when credit is essential. They prey on desperate consumers by billing fees prior to success, wind up doing little to help, and waste consumers' funds. If a credit restoration company agrees to clean up a consumer's credit before ever laying their eyes on it, that is a sign to run the other way. If their fee is not based on success, there is less motivation to work hard for the consumer. Credit restoration should be used when consumers are out of financial stress and on the road to more prosperous times. This is the last step of recovery from financial trauma. Credit restoration would cost her over $2,800, and if she had a new late payment in the process (which she would have, because she was having trouble paying her bills), her score would drop dramatically. Whatever payment she made to us would be money thrown out the window. One new late payment decreases the score anywhere from twenty to one hundred points, depending on how high the score is prior to the new late. She can't refinance her mortgage loan, since the house was worth much less than her current mortgage, and her credit was so bad that the banks would not approve her anyway. She already tried for a loan modification and could not get approved.

Debt consolidation, which is often handled through nonprofit companies, would have reduced her interest on credit card debt. She would then pay the creditors small monthly payments through the consolidation company over a longer period of time. Her $50,000 debt would become $65,000, with the interest and new length of payment plan to her creditors. It could take five to ten years to pay off the debt. After finishing the program, she would need credit repair, which would cost about $2,800 additionally and take up to a year. Her total cost would be around $67,500, and the time factor could be five to ten years.

Using debt settlement, a company would settle the debt for a reduced amount (usually 40 percent of debt). This was out of the question, since she needed the funds to pay her creditors in one shot and did not have savings. She would have needed between $20,000 and $30,000 available to pay the credit card debt once it was settled. If she had the lump sum funds, she would have had to pay taxes on the $20,000 to $30,000 she saved, since it is viewed as income. In some cases, a good CPA could find a way out of the tax liability, depending on the losses the consumer had that year. Then, she would need to clean up her credit, which would cost her $2,800. So she would be paying in total—if she saved $30,000 and went to a typical debt settlement company (they would have charged her 15 percent of what they saved her): $20,000 for debt + $4,500 to the debt settlement company + $8,400 to the IRS if she was in a 28 percent tax bracket. Total paid: $32,900 + $2,800 to clean up credit = $35,700. This whole process would probably take one to two years.

If she sold the house in a short sale, she would be forgiven the amount the bank lost (check with your CPA about tax laws, since they change often).

- mortgage $300,000
- sells house for $160,000
- government forgives the tax on the $140,000 income bank forgave on her mortgage (check with your CPA to see if this would apply to you)
- goes into bankruptcy and pays $1,500 to $1,800 for attorney
- wipes out debt of $50,000 to credit card companies
- one to two years later, she can start credit restoration and clean up her credit, which costs her approximately $2,800 and takes six to twelve months to complete

Her total cost is about $4,500 to wipe out $190,000 of debt and start over. It took her four more months and cost her another $4,000 since she tried to stay afloat and pay her mortgage and credit card debt until she was willing to accept the bankruptcy option. It was the stigma of bankruptcy that initially stopped her. You can get a mortgage two to three years after bankruptcy, or sooner (speak to your mortgage professional). We found out later that she had used the increasing value on her house, before the market crashed, to take out a loan of $60,000. She really made money on her home.

Bankruptcy Example

An architect owns a home that has held its value, but his mortgage was still almost the value of his home. His salary went from $175,000 to $40,000 in the last year. He has $85,000 in credit card debt and had late payments in the past eight months. His interest rates with the creditors skyrocketed, and they refused to decrease them. He is struggling to pay the credit card payments and lives under incredible stress and fear. He never thought he could go to bankruptcy since he owned a home. He is the only income earner in the family and has two little kids in private school. He came to us for advice, and we connected him with a bankruptcy attorney and a possible loan modification as well. This was his best option, and he was relieved he didn't have to give up his home.

Debt Settlement Example

I spoke with an elderly man whose business had just dissolved. He has a home with a small loan and large value. He has savings, but his wife was ill with a chronic disease, and he was suffering from depression. He owed $40,000 in credit card debt and had a 750 credit score. He and his wife were not earning any income. After speaking with him for a while, I learned he did not need his credit and was not concerned about a reduction in his scores. He was not a candidate for bankruptcy, and it made sense for us to negotiate his debt. The creditors would not even speak to us until he was four months late and his credit score dropped. It was a tough situation for him and his wife, since they were bombarded with harassing phone calls (even after telling their creditors to stop calling them) day and night. They thought it over, and we were able to save them about $24,000. They were very happy and relieved at the end of the process. It did cost them $2,000 for our services and the taxes paid on their savings to the IRS. Remember, each situation is different in terms of taxes paid and must be discussed with your CPA.

Loan Modification Example

A professional with a family owns a home worth upwards of $1,000,000 on Long Island. After owning the home for a year, he took a loan on the increased value to renovate (about twenty-nine months ago). He has a salary of over $250,000 and is the only income earner in his family. He called to ask about debt settlement after talking with a debt settlement company that called him. He owed over $175,000. The debt settlement company most likely found him on a list the CRAs sold to companies seeking high-debt individuals. He was barely covering his mortgage and having a difficult time paying his credit card debt. His interest rates on the credit card debt were hiked up, because his balances were very high if not at the limits. He was told by a debt settlement company that his credit would not be ruined, even though he would have to stop paying his debt, and he would probably not have to pay taxes on his savings. He would have to put money into a bank account the debt settlement company controlled. The goal was to save enough money for the settlement company to pay the creditors 40 percent of what he owed. The settlement company took their fee upfront, and when he had enough in the special savings account, they would begin to negotiate his debt.

Most of this was false. If you don't pay your bills on time, you will have late payments on your credit report. End of story. He really needed to look into getting a loan modification first, since the amount of his mortgage was, most likely, more than his property value. If he had many settled accounts with late payments, he may not have qualified for the loan modification. We referred him to an attorney to discuss his mortgage situation and advised him against debt settlement until he examined the loan modification option first. He also needed to find out what the tax ramifications would be if he had more than $100,000 added to his $250,000 income after his credit card debt was settled for less.

Debt Consolidation Example
A woman earning $100,000 had $30,000 of credit card debt and very high expenses. Her balances are very close to limits, and some were over the limits. She wants to pay her creditors but can't handle the high interest rates and increased minimum payments. She owns a condo in Manhattan with a little equity and piece of property upstate with a value of $30,000. She was denied a loan against her property because of low scores caused by her high balances on revolving credit card debt. And although her property was on the market, it was not selling. Debt consolidation may be the best choice for her, since her interest rates could be reduced to 6 percent rather than the 23 percent she is currently paying. She will pay the debt consolidation company a small fee plus a reduced monthly payment, which they will deliver to her creditors.

It is important that she knows the debt consolidation company may make her reduced monthly payments late or put a mark on her credit profile stating she is in a debt consolidation plan. This mark negatively affects the scores. She can ask the nonprofit debt consolidation company to keep this info off her credit profile and to make sure payments are made on time, but there is no guarantee either will occur. We have seen the scores drop dramatically because of these marks. The credit can always be cleaned up when she gets a handle on her debt. If she is saving 17 percent interest on her $30,000, and her payments are not drawn out for ten years, debt consolidation could be a good choice in this situation.

These examples show the available options and the types of struggles we see in this economy. One thing we find again and again is the misconception that a bankruptcy is so much worse for credit than anything else. If you have excellent credit scores and have a new late payment, the score can drop seventy to over one hundred points. If you continue to have more late payments, the score will drop further. If your score is already very low, a bankruptcy will not drop it much lower. Credit scores are driven by what is happening now. As the late payments and the bankruptcy age, the score increases. Scores will increase quicker for a late payment than a bankruptcy. We can also improve the credit a year after bankruptcy.

Once your credit scores are low, it is pointless to worry about the score if you can't pay your bills and are having trouble with basic necessities. Credit scores can always be improved. It is sad to see a person struggling to pay credit card debt before feeding themselves and their families. Bankruptcy is there for a reason and can be a great tool in difficult times. But there are some professions that will not hire a person with a bankruptcy on their record, so when seeking information, make sure to ask about this possibility and how it relates to your career. It is important for consumers to seek information before deciding to make any move forward. Speak with a bankruptcy attorney, a debt consolidation company, a mortgage and loan modification expert, a good real estate agent for short sale info, and an ethical credit restoration firm. The information they can provide is very important to making an educated decision.

Chapter Seven
Credit Monitoring and Identity Protection

People are generally confused about how to protect their credit and identity. There are more than a few ways to protect your credit, and it is important to know which is best for you.

There are three types of fraud:

Identity Theft—the use of personal identification information to commit credit fraud or other crimes.

Assuming Identity — long-term victimization of your identification information.

Fraud Sprees—unauthorized charges on existing accounts.

Some of the ways in which we become a victim to this costly, time-consuming, and infuriating crime are through our mailbox, lost or stolen credit cards, our trash, unsolicited telephone calls or e-mails, and personal records. And, we may not even notice someone looking over our shoulder while we are in the midst of an ATM or other transaction, yet this person may be taking note of important information, such as a password. Having a criminal find your personal records through a third party or stealing your wallet may be out of your control, but there are many ways in which you can be proactive to protect your identity and credit. Having a lock on your mailbox, whether you live in a secluded area or on a busy highway, is essential in this day and age. Always keep a shredder next to the area where you look through your mail. Shred everything you discard, especially credit card offers with checks attached. Do not carry your Social Security card. That number can open the doorway to all kinds of fraudulent activity. Don't carry all your credit cards in your wallet, and keep a list of the ones you have with you on your cell phone (excluding the account numbers). When your wallet or purse has been stolen, you want to make sure you know what you must cancel. Canceling all your cards because you are unsure of what you had could cause more damage to your credit than necessary. Be careful to avoid intrusion into your personal space when in the midst of transactions. Do not give any personal information to creditors via telephone or e-mail if the contact is unsolicited. If you want to be certain about their authenticity, get the company's phone number through a third party, and call to verify on your own. Always check all charges on your credit card statements and immediately inform creditors if there are items you do not recognize. Sometimes, the corporate name of a business is different from the name of the store where you shop or from which you ordered. You may suddenly recognize the charge when you get more information about where and when the purchase was made.

Data Breach

Data breach is what happens when an organization or person has information stolen or lost that could be used to steal their identity or use credit in an unauthorized manner. This includes financial records, medical records, and student records. This information could be taken through hacking, files accidentally thrown away or discarded, and stolen laptops. We have even heard of banks that left records in bags for the garbage pickup. Once, we got a phone call from a real estate agent who left a briefcase containing records of ten potential buyers in a taxi. These records included Social Security numbers, addresses, and bank account numbers. If this happens, it is important to put a fraud alert on your credit reports and to monitor your credit closely.

Account Takeover

When a consumer is a victim of account takeover, it means that a thief has gathered existing credit account information or bank account data and is making charges to the consumer's accounts. Consumers usually find out when they check their monthly statements or see balances that don't make sense.

Fraudulent Charges on Existing Credit Cards

Credit card fraud comes in many forms, one of which is active credit card charges. We all need to protect our credit scores and financial life from this potentially debilitating crime. When thinking about credit fraud, many individuals think of accounts being opened without authorization. This is one type of fraud, but there are others that are subtler and could be harder to detect. How many consumers read every transaction on their credit card statements?

Many have been victimized after using their credit card at a store, restaurant, gas station, or pharmacy, and later that month or even longer, realize that many unauthorized charges have been made on the card. Have you ever given your credit card to an individual and felt a tinge of reluctance? Something about that person or transaction didn't feel right, or you just had a gut feeling something was wrong. If that happens, it is best to walk away. Many individuals have had fraud committed against them with their existing credit cards. It seems that the majority of consumers did not notice until long afterward. The longer it takes to figure out this fraud occurred, the less likely the creditor will believe it is legitimate. To protect against this type of fraud, all charges and transactions must be reviewed on every statement. For most consumers, it takes just a few minutes to do this, and it could save a lot of trouble down the road.

When fraud is detected, it is most important to call the creditor immediately. We have seen numerous situations where fraud was committed and the consumer did not report it for years. Consumers just discarded the charges they felt were not theirs and did not pay them. This is not a problem that will just go away; it needs to be confronted and investigated.

CREDIT CARD FRAUD DOS AND DON'TS FROM THE FTC WEBSITE:

Do:

- Sign your cards as soon as they arrive.

- Carry your cards separately from your wallet, in a zippered compartment, a business card holder, or another small pouch.

- Keep a record of your account numbers, their expiration dates, and the phone number and address of each company in a secure place.

- Keep an eye on your card during the transaction, and get it back as quickly as possible.

- Void incorrect receipts.

- Destroy carbons.

- Save receipts to compare with billing statements.

- Open bills promptly and reconcile accounts monthly, just as you would your checking account.

- Report any questionable charges promptly and in writing to the card issuer.

- Notify card companies in advance of a change in address.

Don't:

- Lend your card(s) to anyone.

- Leave cards or receipts lying around.

- Sign a blank receipt. When you sign a receipt, draw a line through any blank spaces above the total.

- Write your account number on a postcard or the outside of an envelope.

Give out your account number over the phone unless you're making the call to a company you know is reputable. If you have questions about a company, check it out with your local consumer protection office or the Better Business Bureau.

Chart from:
Consumer Protection website, January 2011, http://www.ftc.gov/bcp/edu/pubs/consumer/credit/cre07.

Fraud Alerts

You have the right to ask that the CRA's place "fraud alerts" in your file so that potential and existing creditors will know you may be a victim of identity theft. A fraud alert can, however, make it more difficult for you to get credit in your name, because your creditors will have to follow certain procedures to protect you. Creditors will have to contact you for approval on new credit before allowing it to be issued. If they cannot reach you, it will be declined. To place a fraud alert on your file, you can call one of the three credit reporting companies. You will have to provide the bureaus with specific proof of identity. Once you apply for this alert with one of the agencies, the other two will be notified automatically to place the same alert.

There are two types of fraud alerts. An initial fraud alert stays on your file for ninety days; an extended fraud alert can stay on your credit file for up to seven years. To file an extended fraud alert, you will be required to provide more documentation, including a report from a federal, state, or local law enforcement agency. You can go to www.ftc.gov/idtheft to learn more about it.

To remove these alerts you must submit written permission with proof of identity to the bureaus.

Security Freeze

A security freeze stops people and companies from having access to your credit. A security freeze stops third parties (except for those exempt by law: the government investigating a crime and creditors with whom consumers have current accounts) from viewing your credit reports and from reporting certain information on them. Having a security freeze placed on your credit profile can inhibit your ability to get a new loan, credit, mortgage, insurance, government services or payments, rental housing, employment, investment, license, cellular telephone, utilities, digital signature, Internet credit card transaction, or other services, including an extension of credit at point of sale. If your name or other personal information changes while you have the security freeze, only you will be able to change it through submission of a written request and proof with the bureaus directly. This is a serious alert and should not be taken lightly. You can get a security freeze by requesting it from the CRAs with proof of identity. There are fees associated with this alert depending on the state in which you live. If you are over a certain age, you may be eligible for a free freeze. Usually, this freeze stays on the report until you authorize its removal in writing; in some states, it stays on the file for seven years. A temporary lift can be requested by the consumer, where the agencies provide you with a pin number, and your creditors will have a specific access code for approval to review your reports. The lifts are usually valid for one to thirty days.

Identity Theft Tools of Protection

1. Credit Monitoring Protection
Many of our clients have asked, since 2006, if credit monitoring is worth having and if we can provide this service. Credit monitoring is a huge business, and with scores so important, it will continue to grow. Credit monitoring offers many positives but does not stop fraud from occurring. It can alert you when

balances change, accounts are opened or closed, or your score fluctuates. It can even offer fraud alerts. It is a way to see what is occurring on your credit daily, weekly, or monthly, depending on the product you choose. We have all seen promotional offers for free monitoring of your credit profile.

A credit monitoring product should charge a monthly fee to watch your credit daily and alert you to a variety of changes:

-Balance changes
-Accounts being opened or closed
-Changes in personal information
-Give consumer the ability to put fraud alerts on credit profile
-Inquiries and reviews of credit conducted

Consumers should also be given an idea what the current status of their credit is in comparison with others in the country. Is it fair, good, great, or poor credit. These updates come via e-mail.

I have studied these services for many years. One of the pluses the monitoring companies talk about is fraud prevention. The only thing a monitoring company can do is alert you when accounts are opened, but it can't prevent fraud. Once it happens, it is already too late. When you begin to see signs of identity theft on your credit report, the damage has already been done. The signs on your credit report are the scars of this crime. It is just as logical as studying for an exam after you fail. Identity theft is a process, and the result of it is seeing accounts on your credit report that do not belong to you. These accounts are usually in default with late payments or have gone to the point of collection or charge-off. If you see accounts that are not yours on your credit profile but they are in good standing, it probably isn't identity theft. If your name is common or a relative has the same, or similar, name, the accounts can be listed with the wrong person.

Credit monitoring cannot protect a consumer from identity theft or credit card fraud. What it can do is alert them when new activity on the credit profile has been generated. This could be accounts opened by the consumer or a thief using the consumer's information to commit fraud. It is true that once the problem is known, it can help consumers to react faster and save some frustration. If a monitoring company provides notices that a creditor is inquiring into the consumer's history, with or without authorization, it is helpful, since they are being notified before the account is opened. The problem is what to do with unauthorized inquiry information. An individual would have to track down the creditor, get someone on the phone who knows what they are talking about, and have them figure out why they inquired into the history. This is a lot of unnecessary work. What can be done to block certain types of fraud is to place a fraud alert on the credit report so that creditors would have to contact the consumer directly by phone for approval. Although this may not allow consumers the option of getting instant credit, it will surely stop identity theft in the form of new accounts. This can be done through credit monitoring companies as well.

Credit monitoring can be a valuable tool, but there are many consumers who do not understand credit in general, and this becomes a problem when using most monitoring products. How will these individuals understand what each alert means and how to handle them? Monitoring companies alert you for various reasons, some being inconsequential. For example, John has a Home Depot account and keeps a balance under $30.00. One month he buys a $300 item, and his alert from the monitoring company states, "A balance on your credit profile has increased 300 percent." He cannot see his exact state of credit at this time without ordering a full, up-to-date credit report (some monitoring products only alert you and do not show full report status). He panics and starts calling all his creditors. After four hours, he realizes it was the Home Depot card and begins to feel an ease of mind. He may spend the $15.00 to purchase his full report again.

If the product isn't clear enough to explain the specifics of the alert, it could do more harm than good. We find most consumers ask us what their alerts really mean. To use a monitoring product well, consumers must understand how to read their credit profile. If they want to have the highest scores, staying abreast of changes in the scoring systems and requirements of creditors in regards to scores is essential. This is a lot to keep up with, and most monitoring products do not give consumers all of this information. I spend most of my workweek and at least four hours a weekend studying these topics to stay current. Imagine how hard it would be for the average consumer. Because of this challenge, we have created a boutique-style credit monitoring product for consumers who do not have the time or inclination to learn the intricacies and subtleties of how scores change. These individuals get personalized service from our credit experts, who take the time to explain what needs to be done to keep scores as high as possible. We keep a watchful eye on changes to the credit files and contact each individual when and if suspicious activity occurs. This product is not necessary for all but a great asset for those who would like to learn about credit and just don't have the time to investigate all the misinformation. These individuals want a trusted source to help them. You can learn more at www.ecsprofessional.com.

2. Protect Your Computer

Hackers control your computer through spyware, viruses, worms, and Trojan horse programs. To protect your computer against these problems, you must use antivirus, anti-spyware and anti-malware software and keep these applications up to date. Always have a firewall that is set up correctly. Change passwords and administrative names often. Keep your wireless networks closed to the public, and shut down your computer when you are not using it.

Never open e-mail spam or any e-mails from addresses you don't recognize. Stay away from opening private, sensitive accounts when using public networks. Don't download free programs without full knowledge they are safe.

3. Identity Theft Insurance and Protection

What does identity theft protection mean? Identity theft protection comes in the form of searching for information and insurance. The insurance aspect usually covers some of the costs for attorneys, investigators, or accountants. It does not cover the actual loss of money for charges incurred on a credit card or accounts that were opened in a consumer's name by the thief. It does not reimburse for the time spent sorting out all of the problems that need to be resolved from this crime. Some policies will reimburse for income lost if there was time taken off from work to fill out police reports, and so on. This reimbursement is a limited amount of money. The definitions of terms in these policies are very general and many of them will not cover New York State. It is unclear why a CPA or investigator would be needed if a consumer were a victim of this crime. It seems that there are departments of the government already doing the investigating. Our tax dollars are paid to cover the Consumer Fraud Divisions, the FBI, and the attorney general. Since we already have paid for these agencies through our taxes, why would we need to pay again to an insurance product? In a majority of instances, these crimes are committed by a family member or someone the consumer knows. If that is the case, these insurance policies will not cover the costs.

Companies like LifeLock state that they scan public records, credit card applications, Social Security card requests, and Internet chat rooms for potentially fraudulent activity. What I have read and heard from consumers is that LifeLock is, for the most part, putting fraud alerts on credit profiles, updating them every ninety days, and opting consumers out of promotional offers for credit cards. Many banks and insurance companies offer products for protecting identity as well. It makes one wonder about their ability to protect a consumer's identity when they are the same companies contacting consumers to warn them of security breaches that they themselves are experiencing. So, if they are making consumers more susceptible to becoming victims in the first place, how can they possibly protect us?

Most of us have seen the commercial featuring the CEO of LifeLock, Todd Davis, who had his Social Security number listed on the side of a bus. He stated how comfortable he felt displaying those numbers to the world, because of his confidence in his company's ability to protect consumers from identity theft. Well, he did become the victim of identity theft after publicly revealing his Social Security number. I found it interesting that under the terms and conditions of their LifeLock product, it states that consumers cannot display their Social Security number publicly. They consider this reckless behavior. Here is the exact wording written under the *conduct* portion of the terms and conditions:

> You will not recklessly disclose or publish your Social Security number or any other Personal Information[26]

It was also surprising to see that all services provided by LifeLock are governed by the laws of Arizona. Do you know what the Arizona laws are? I don't. So, I guess consumers need an attorney in Arizona who can really explain how these laws would affect them if their identity was stolen and they needed LifeLock to cover damages. Here is the exact quote:

---

26 LifeLock website, October 2010, http://www.lifelock.com/about-us/about-lifelock/privacy-policy.

This Agreement and any Service provided here under will be governed by the laws of the State of Arizona, without regard to any laws that would direct the choice of another state's laws and, where applicable, to be governed by the federal laws of the United States.

If a consumer has their identity stolen while using LifeLock he or she is assured there will be coverage up to $1,000,000 for a lifetime. This $1,000,000 is not for direct losses due to the theft but for attorney or professional fees, such as investigation fees. LifeLock states these fees will be paid based on, "their judgment." That is pretty general and gives them a lot of room to deny payment. This is an exact quote:

LifeLock will retain and pay for those third party professional services that are reasonably necessary in LifeLock's judgment to assist you in restoring losses or recovering your lost out-of-pocket expenses caused by such fraud. LifeLock will pay such third parties up to a maximum of one million dollars ($1,000,000) over your lifetime for all such fraud incidents.[27]

So, in the light of day, this company, which seems to be the most highly recommended, doesn't have much faith in its own abilities.

All in all, credit monitoring can be very helpful. Consumers who choose these products must pay attention to the alerts and learn how to navigate the monitoring site and tools. If a consumer does not give the attention needed to make these

---

[27] LifeLock website, October 2010, http://www.lifelock.com/about-us/about-lifelock/terms-and-conditions.

products of value, it is better to order credit reports and scores quarterly. This way, they can be analyzed for suspicious activity every three months. The insurance that I have investigated seems to be quite vague in terms of what it covers, so I would not spend extra money on it. If it is offered with a monitoring product, it can't hurt, since it is included in the fees.

Ending Statement

With this book, consumers can get an overall knowledge of how credit and scores work. The information contained can help consumers increase their scores by hundreds of points. Consumers learn what is detrimental and essential to great credit scores, how to prepare credit prior to getting a loan or mortgage, and the unknown pitfalls that most overlook. How joint accounts and divorce can damage credit and set consumers back from meeting their goals. When financial stress affects credit and scores, what are the necessary steps in moving forward, and what should be of highest importance? There are choices available to those facing financial problems relating to real estate values, loss of income, medical problems, and more. This book can help consumers live a better life financially and have more opportunities available to them. It is important to remember that the rules of credit do change frequently. There will be new editions of this book every few years to make sure consumers have the most current information about credit and scores. You can always find the most current articles located on our website, www.northshoreadvisory.com.

www.ingramcontent.com/pod-product-compliance
Lightning Source LLC
Chambersburg PA
CBHW022000170526
45157CB00003B/1075